Lemonade Stand Selling

Praise For Lemonade Stand Selling

"**Lemonade Stand Selling** uses simple, easy to understand, down to earth language and examples to help dispel the myths many people believe about the sales process. It also includes sound direction for those who need to master sales. Even if you consider yourself a seasoned salesperson, there are lessons you can learn in the pages of this excellent book." **Dr. Tony Alessandra, Hall-of-Fame Motivational Speaker and author of** *The Platinum Rule* **and** *Charisma* **books**

"Reading this book is like getting sales advice from a good friend - who also happens to be an expert sales coach! It's encouraging and easy to understand with plenty of examples to show you the way. If you're struggling with your sales, this may just be the pick-me-up you need." **Tina Lo Sasso, Managing Editor, SalesDog.com**

"Diane's work is to the point and so applicable. Her rich use of examples gives the reader chances to put the information to work for their environment right now. These results oriented pages will lift your business." **Kordell Norton, Speaker, Author, Graphic Facilitator**

"At the core of every successful organization is the ability to sell - nothing happens in this world until somebody sells something. This is essentially Diane's message, and she conveys that message superbly. This is a must read book for all small business owners and entrepreneurs - and, I do mean MUST." **Jonathan Farrington, Chairman of The Sales Corporation**

Praise For Lemonade Stand Selling

"Forget all the fancy-schmancy how-to sales books; the ones with the nine steps and the complicated diagrams. Helbig reminds us all that we've known how to sell since we were about five years old. This is stuff we've all always known to work when it comes to selling. She simply reminds us to DO it!" **Debbie Fay, Bespeak Presentation Solutions**

"Sales isn't scary or difficult. It is, however, necessary for success. Diane provides the reader with a no nonsense approach to the sales process that is based in common sense. This book is essential for every small business owner who has to sell and provides a workable sales plan that gets results simply by reading these pages." **Hal Becker, Author and Sales Consultant**

"Diane has written an awesome, down to earth real world book, filled with great illustrations, stories and practical suggestions, she 'sold me'! Whether a novice or veteran salesperson, if you want to improve your skills and make more money, it's a must read." **El Laflamme, CLP, Author of "Green Side Up - straight talk on growing & operating a profitable landscaping business!" www.harvestlandscapeconsulting. com**

"Full of practical sales tips interwoven with real life examples. This book will allow you to exceed your own expectations." **Clayton Shold, President, Salesopedia**

Praise For Lemonade Stand Selling

"I like how Diane gets right to the point about the importance of information gathering during the sales process. She also discusses the importance of asking the right questions and that the "first" problem the prospect mentions is rarely the real or most important one. I highly recommend this book for anyone that needs either a sales "tune-up" or is just starting out in a sales career." **Joel Libava, President, Franchise Selection Specialists, Inc.**

Lemonade Stand Selling

Accelerate Your Small Business Growth

By Diane Helbig

Thomson, Georgia

Sales Gravy Press
The Sales Book Publisher™
P.O. Box 1389
Thomson, GA 30824

Published by Sales Gravy Press
Printed in the United States of America

Cover Design: Dave Blaker

First Edition

ISBN-13: 978-0-9818004-6-2
ISBN-10: 0-9818004-6-7

Table of Contents

Foreword by Anita Campbell

One of the most terrifying parts of leaving the corporate world and starting your own business is the sudden realization that no money will be coming in the door unless you bring it in.

Eeek! YOU are now responsible for sales.

The old saying "Nothing happens until somebody sells something" takes on alarming new meaning when that somebody is you.

I'm not kidding when I use the word "terrifying" because that's often the reaction when reality hits you. That was my reaction when I started my business.

Of course, if you've been in sales your entire career you'll probably smile at that thought. Why would sales terrify anyone, you wonder? But then, if you're a sales professional you probably don't need this book, either.

This is a book for the rest of us. It's a book for those of us faced with a burning desire to grow our businesses – but uncomfortable with the process of having to ask clients for money.

You likely were quite successful at whatever you've done in your career to date. You probably have a long list of accomplishments. But chances are, whatever roles you've had and were so good at, didn't involve being the one to ask for the order. You were not responsible for sales.

Now, though, as the owner of your own business, asking for the order is everything. You're painfully aware, each day as you wake up, that if you don't get paid, you won't survive in business for yourself for very long.

And unless you're just starting up your business today, by now you've also tasted the sweet heady high of actually getting the order. There's no more satisfying feeling as a business owner than to close a big deal, or to see dollars rolling in regularly to your cash register or bank account.

Why do you think so many people save and frame the first dollar they ever made in their businesses?

Making a sale is a huge accomplishment. Few things are as motivating as getting confirmation, in cold hard cash, that others are willing to pay you for whatever product or service you provide.

If any of this strikes a chord with you, then I know you. You're not the type of business owner who will be satisfied with just scraping by. You want more – you want success. And that's where this book comes in.

This is the kind of book I wish I'd had early on when I started my business. Because it's really about overcoming fear.

Fear is your worst enemy as a business owner. Fear plays with your head. It chips away at your confidence. It paralyzes you with self-doubt.

To be successful, you have to overcome fear and all the baggage it saddles you with. As a business owner, you need to feel invincible as you start each work day. You need to feel like David taking on Goliath. You need to feel that you know exactly what to do today – this day – to ask for and get the order!

One thing I've learned: to get to that invincible feeling you must master the sales process. When you feel in control of how to get clients and payments, your confidence will skyrocket.

This book lays out a sales system designed expressly for the small business owner/salesperson. It breaks down common scenarios, step by step, into techniques just about anyone can employ.

Diane Helbig helps you develop a marketing and sales process for your business that's as simple as running a lemonade stand. If you know what moves to make in sales and marketing, fear evaporates. Then you'll be armed with the essential skills you need to take on each day with enthusiasm … ready to seize it to sell something … to "make something happen."

Introduction

So you own a business. Maybe you started from scratch, maybe you bought a franchise, or maybe you bought into a business already in motion. Whatever your launch pad, congratulations! You are to be celebrated. Business ownership is not for the feint of heart but for the courageous, the adventurous, and the optimistic. The journey is full of rewards and challenges.

I have worked in the business world for many years, operating my coaching practice for the last three and a half years. Throughout this time, I've encountered too many small business owners who struggle with their sales and marketing process. The reasons vary, but the basis tends to be a lack of experience and knowledge. That deficit creates fear and fear creates paralysis.

If you are a small business owner wondering what I'm talking about – here it is. To be successful you must master sales. No worries! As you read this book you'll realize that this doesn't mean you'll be pushy, obnoxious, soliciting family and friends, or any other dreaded vision you have of "sales."

Actually, it's as simple as running a lemonade stand. Remember when you were a child? If you had a lemonade stand you didn't think about sales – you simply set out to sell cups of lemonade. Somehow you knew what to do. Maybe you watched an older sibling or neighbor run their own stand. Maybe it just came naturally.

It is my opinion that the reason you could forge ahead and sell your lemonade is because you had no fear. You didn't spend time thinking and worrying about what to do or how to sell. You just did it.

And it wasn't hard, was it? Not at all. It was actually pretty simple and basic. Well, that is the essence of sales. There is no magic, no difficult landscape to traverse. You will realize as you read through this book that sales is simple, as simple as having a lemonade stand and selling your lemonade.

We are going to spend time working on the steps of a successful sales process. You may find that you have some of the areas under control. No problem. Just move on to the next step. The intention is to help you navigate the seemingly difficult waters of sales and marketing successfully. The goal is to leave you with the ability to put these ideas into practice and create a strategy that works for you.

Believe it or not, I fought the idea of being a salesperson for a full year before giving in to my boss (the president of the company). Once I figured out a system that worked for me, I enjoyed a successful sales career for many years. I learned a lot during that time. The biggest lesson I learned was that sales is really simple. It's about you being you and sharing information about something that matters to someone else. Hey, isn't that the same thing as selling lemonade? Yes it is!

While sales is work, it is as simple as that lemonade stand you had as a child. So, don't let anyone complicate it for you. We're going to review all of the basics of sales, and you will see that it never goes beyond the most basic of principles. You may even find yourself saying "But, of course!"

If you do – great! That means you get it. If you find that you aren't getting it, step back and look to see if you are making it more complicated than it has to be.

And remember, while there are certain things you must do as a business owner, how you do it is all about who you are. I have found that those who experience the deepest long-term success are the people who are true to their authentic selves. This is because they are successful as THEY define it! They aren't living their lives or running their businesses as others expect them to. They aren't trying to fit into someone else's box. They've created their own world, so it works for them. They've also created their own sales strategy – one that is simple, personal, and authentic.

As we explore the various aspects of the sales process consider how you can incorporate the steps in a way that will work for you. Take the 'must have' parts of sales and create your own sales strategy.

Remember this, the entire process begins with a belief in yourself and your product or service. The people who can get out there and sell are the people who truly believe they have something of value to offer.

Well, you went into business for a reason, right? You thought you had something someone else needed or wanted. Hang on to that. It can take time to build energy around your sales process. No one walks out the door and is an instant success. It takes a plan, time, and perseverance.

I had the pleasure of hearing Debbie Fields of Mrs. Field's Cookies speak at a conference. She told the story of the day she opened her first store. She stood there with a tray of cookies just waiting for people to come in. She quickly realized that no one was coming and thought to herself, 'If I don't do something, my business is over.' So she walked out the door with that same tray of cookies and found customers. She took action and made something happen. That something turned into a multi-million dollar business.

Remember that story as you navigate the sales process. Everyone is a little scared. That's normal. However, those who are successful are those who have taken that fear and turned it into action. Those who are successful are also those who keep it simple – Lemonade Stand Simple –.

Throughout the book we are going to follow Matt, the print broker. Matt finds out what printed materials his clients need and then shops for the best printer in terms of quality and price. Watch how Matt handles the situations he encounters. Even though your industry may be different, the rules that apply are not. You should be able to learn from Matt.

Chapter One

Identity, Clarity, Value

What is it that you sell and why would someone buy it?

Kate decides she wants to be a Virtual Assistant. She's read a lot about this field and believes it fits right into her skills, lifestyle, and needs. She puts on paper the services she'll provide – newsletter creation, sales letter creation and distribution, social media profile setup and continued presence, and sales literature creation.

From her research into this field she determines her pricing structure and performance terms. She knows what she will charge and how she will get the work done. She includes in her plan details for communicating with her clients regarding jobs, billing, timeframes, and other expectations.

Kate has also listed the benefits of her services to her clients. She has real clarity about what she is selling and why it has value.

The real beginning of the sales process is having a solid idea of what it is you are selling. When I was a child I had a lemonade stand. Well, actually I had a lemonade and candy stand. I had determined that I wanted to offer more than just a drink. I wanted to have some candy to sell as well. So I set out creating the products. You could equate it to a manufacturing company. I created the candy and the lemonade I sold.

But that wasn't the end of defining 'it.' Once I had the products, I had to decide how I was packaging them, what their value was, and what the pricing would be. You see, I had to really define the saleable product. Until I did that, I couldn't advertise, market, or sell. I had to be able to speak about it so that others would understand it.

This is the first step in the sales process for YOUR lemonade stand. The goal is to craft the product package so you will have clarity about what it is and what its value is. If you offer a service rather than a product, define your scope of work.

First, write down what the product is – physically. If there is more than one product, list each of them. If it's a service you'll be providing, write down all that is entailed in the offering. In other words, the process you will go through, what you will and won't do, the timeline, and the expected result. Once again if you offer more than one service or you have packages of services, create the detail for each.

This is a critical step. You must know the scope of the work you will do. This is an area that can really trip up a small business owner turned salesperson. Before you know it you'll be neck-deep in non-revenue generating activities. Or, you won't be able to start an effective sales strategy because you won't have a clear idea of what you offer. Moreover, until you have clarity, you won't truly understand the value of your product or service.

Example: John offers website design and construction. He has a clear idea of the time it takes to create his websites and has designated three categories of sites. From this he has been able to attach a price to each category. Great, right? Wrong. John suddenly realizes that he is spending a lot of time in the planning and discussion phase with his clients. Some of them never land on what they want, while it takes others several conversations and redesigns to finally capture the desired outcome. All that time is non-revenue generating because John didn't include that time in his pricing structures.

So, John is spending a huge amount of time planning instead of producing. All on his own dime. The solution is this – John offers a one-hour consultation free of charge. He provides a detailed spec sheet for the client to fill out so the time is used effectively. After that hour, the meter starts and John is now charging for his time. This results in several positive changes:

1. He is now being paid for this time so it is revenue generating.
2. His clients make solid decisions during the free hour to help reduce their cost.
3. John now has more projects going that are generating revenue because his clients are not stuck in the planning phase.
4. John is able to do more for more clients, increasing his client base and reputation.

Think about your own experience.
- Do you provide a lot of free consulting?
- Do your clients have difficulty pulling the trigger and starting projects?
- Do you find yourself having a nebulous idea of what you offer?
- Do you ever find yourself at odds with your customer? For example, you had one thought and they had a com-

pletely different understanding? If so, it's because you didn't have clarity about your product offering. The problem? You left room for your client to develop their own belief.

Let's eliminate that problem

Now that you've detailed WHAT it is, put into words WHY your product or service has value. Why do you think it's valuable?

Remember, you went into business because you thought you had something that other people needed or wanted. You must have had a reason. Get it on paper. That's only the beginning of the value question.

Next put into words why others see value in it. Why do they believe they need or want it? Why do people buy that thing? What is the problem it solves or prevents? There's a strong belief in the sales world that people buy to either eliminate or avoid pain. That 'pain' depends on to whom you are selling.

Think about what you sell in terms of how it eases or prevents pain for your client.

If you sell to businesses and organizations, then pain can be: cumbersome processes, inability to track inventory, employment issues, mobility, etc. Pain is really anything that makes a businessperson's life difficult.

If you sell something directly to consumers, then pain is anything that makes a person's life difficult or imperfect. Think about what you sell in terms of how it eases or prevents pain for your client. If you believe that, then your product or service has to solve or prevent that problem.

If you get stuck here, ask your current clients what makes your product or service valuable to them. If you are just launching your product or service, and don't have any clients, find people who buy this product or service elsewhere and survey them. Ask people you know why they would buy it.

Regardless of how you gather the information, your goal is to have a better understanding of what it is about your product or service that makes people want to spend money for it.

Speaking of money, now's the time to determine the price you will charge. It's important to establish appropriate pricing. Appropriate pricing is not too low or too high. It is a combination of a couple of factors. You don't want to undervalue your product/service, nor let others undervalue it. Why? Because the message it sends is that you don't believe in your product or service. When you let someone beat you up on price, they are telling you that they don't value your product/service. Even worse, you are telling them you don't value it either.

As an aside, let me just say that those people who beat you up on price are also the people who create the most work for you. They don't see value in what you are offering. I submit to you that you don't want to do business with them.

You also don't want to overvalue your product/service. When you overprice you lose credibility and sincerity – two things critical to success in business.

Now let's revisit pricing. How much is your prospect willing to pay for your product/service? Components of their decision may be:

1. **Market trends** – What is the going rate? Do some research and determine what the rate ranges are currently for your product or service. Try to compare apples to apples as much as possible. However, areas where you see major differences, indicate where you are differentiated or your competition is. In other words, if you offer a significantly higher value that

you can point to, that is your differentiator. If your research shows you companies offering significantly more than you do within the same price range, that is their differentiator. Either way, it's good to know what you are up against.

2. **Need/desire** – Remember, this is the value your prospect sees. You can have the greatest idea in the world, but if people don't see the need for it, they aren't going to buy it – no matter how much it costs. There has to be a market for your product or service.

3. **Added benefits of working with you** – Can you articulate those benefits? This is what sets you apart – where your edge comes from. It is said that people buy the person first, the product second, and the company third. So, what is it about you that makes people want to do business with you? Unsure? Ask your current clients, former associates, peers, etc.

When I was doing my coach training, one of the assignments was to ask five people who knew me well why I would make a good coach. I can tell you the answers were fascinating and helped me realize my value. I learned the things about me that were my differentiators. Those things that made me different from every other business coach out there.

Well, there is something about you or your business that sets you apart. Whether it's a particular product or an extra service you tack on to your base product, you have something that separates you from everyone else in your industry. It may be as simple as your attention to detail, or your commitment to your clients. Find it; own it. It does matter.

The other side of value is the value you receive from performing the service or selling the product. At what rate is it worth it to you to provide your product/service? In other words, is there a point below which you won't go? A point where it doesn't feel good; doesn't pay the bills? How much do you want to make? Is it reasonable? Is it realistic?

Let's say you are an artist and you sell handmade, silk scarves. You've taken a look at how long it takes you to create a scarf – the number of hours needed. You've added into that time the amount of time you spend in the sales cycle along with the costs to you of marketing your products. When you divide it all up by scarf, you'd have to sell them for $200.00 each. That is the cost below which you can not go. Below $200.00 it isn't worth your time and energy. Now you map that cost against what the market will bear to see if it is viable.

Case in Point

Matt the print broker, offers customized monthly calendars. The client can select the pictures that will be included per month. If it is not stock photography – but rather specific pictures of the client's products, there is a cost involved for Matt to obtain those pictures.

Because these are custom made calendars there is a lot of individual work that goes into them. Matt determines that the price must be $15.00 each with a $100.00 setup fee to make it worth his while to sell and create these calendars.

He now has to float that to prospective clients to find out if they have such a need or desire for these calendars that they are willing to pay that price. If yes, then it is a good deal. If no, then Matt has to decide to take this product off of his menu. People aren't going to buy it for the price he has established. And he can't lower the price because then it isn't worth it to him.

When you know what it's worth to you, and you can describe the value to your prospect, they'll see the cost as reasonable. Now you have your pricing platform.

Simple Cents:

Don't undercut your price just to get business. This is a no-win situation for everyone involved. You won't be happy creating the product or performing the service and that displeasure will show up in your performance. Even though your client is getting a lower price, they won't be happy either because the quality will be less. When they wanted a lower price, they wanted the same level of quality – just for less money. You can do real damage to your reputation by handling a situation this way.

Can you see it coming together? Is the picture getting clearer? Great! Let's move on.

Chapter Two
Marketing

How do you spread the word?

Hank decides that he wants to open up a craft shop. He's organized a handful of local artisans who are excited about having their items displayed and sold at his store. Hank has done all of his upfront work. He knows how he will get the items, what he will charge, where his shop will be. He gets set up and realizes he has to let people know he is open for business.

So, Hank creates a flyer and has about a thousand printed. He then canvasses the area leaving flyers on car windshields and on doors. He also sends a press release to the local media letting them know about his grand opening.

In addition to these efforts, Hank has made sure the artisans are spreading the word in their circles. Part of his marketing effort is to create word of mouth buzz about his shop. Hank is spreading the word.

Remember your lemonade stand when you were young? How did you get the message out? Did you create big signs and hold them up as cars drove by? Maybe you yelled at the cars or took flyers door to door. Whatever your method, you were marketing.

Now that you know WHAT you offer and have identified the specific benefits, you are ready to craft your marketing. Marketing is the process through which you deliver your message.

Start with answering this question: What do I want my prospective clients to know about my product or service?

The answer should speak to the benefits you've defined in Chapter 1. So, be careful. Many small business owners have all kinds of things that are important to them. They have a burning desire to share it. Unfortunately, it usually isn't of interest to their prospects.

Example: Marla sells tankless water heaters. Marla is well versed in how they are installed and the intricacies of how they work. She marvels at this and enjoys talking about it. So, this is the information Marla focused on in her marketing material. The problems with this approach are:

- It is very detailed and wordy so no one reads it
- Her material says nothing about the result of the system – ie: the benefits
- She has failed to engage her prospects

If you overload your prospects with information that is not relevant to them, they will not give you the chance to get to the stuff that IS relevant to them. This is why we spent time on value. Speak to the value, the end result, the benefit to your prospect. THAT is what they care about.

The goal of any marketing effort is to peak the interest of

your prospect so they want to learn more. It should be concise, pithy, intriguing, and most of all it should speak to their interests – not to your interests.

Remember, marketing is the vehicle you use to get your message to your prospect. It is one aspect of prospecting.

The next question is "what marketing vehicles make sense for my business?" There are various avenues for marketing and it is easy to get caught up in unproductive methods. The options are endless: from phone directories to the internet; from ad boards to magazine ads. But, what is right for your product or service and your audience?

Example: My target market is small business. I was approached by an ad salesperson for a local magazine. At first glance, it might seem that advertising in a local magazine is a good idea. Upon further investigation of that magazine, it became apparent that all of the advertising was Business-to-Consumer. The readership is homeowners. When you read the articles and the ads, you see that they are all geared toward the individual - not business.

So, is that the right venue for me? No, it isn't. If I am going to advertise in a magazine, it should be one that is read by small business owners and entrepreneurs. It should be one where the circulation is to businesses, not homes.

You have some decisions to make that are directly related to your target market. Who are they and where are they? Where can you market in a way that they will see your message? Should your approach be high touch or high tech, or some combination of the two? Knowing who and where your target market is will help you narrow down the methods that make sense for you.

Having a website is a critical aspect of marketing. A website provides you with a presence 24-7-365. It works when you are sleeping; it provides some level of credibility; it gives you someplace to direct people; in some cases, it can be revenue generating.

Don't think for a minute that marketing has to be expensive. There are many low or no cost ways to market your product or service. Some examples are the following:

- Use your **voicemail message** to share promotional information about your company. Instead of the traditional 'We can't come to the phone right now. Please leave a message,' say something like, 'Sorry we missed you. We're meeting with a client right now. Did you know we have widgets on sale this month? Visit our website for more information. And don't forget to leave a message! We're eager to speak with you.'
- Send **greeting cards** off season and non-holidays. People expect to get cards for the usual events, but not the unusual. It's a way to stand out.
- Offer your product or service as a giveaway at **networking events or charity functions**. Many organizations look for silent auction and raffle items. What methods yield the best results for your industry?
- Use your **signature** on your email to promote something about your business. Most people have their contact information in their signature. You can add a statement about a promotion you are offering or something about your product or service.
- **Article Marketing** is a great way to direct attention to your website. You can write articles about your industry that are NOT self-promoting. Then submit them to article submission websites like www.ezinearticles.com and www.ideamarketers.com. There are numerous submission sites. The best bet is to Google 'article submission websites' and investigate the list. Submission is free on most sites. The value here is that you are positioning yourself as an expert in your field and your author

bio has a link to your website. People all over the world are looking for good content so you'll find your articles spreading out over the internet as people take them to share. Remember, your website link goes with the article giving you added, free exposure.

- **Blogging** is another way to market. You can create your own blog where you can talk about anything that has to do with your business and industry. Here you can post promotions as well. In addition to having your own blog you can comment on other people's blogs. This is another free way of gaining exposure for your business. When you comment on someone else's blog you are showing their audience that you are an expert in your field. And remember, there will be a link to your website when you post.

- **Getting press** is one of the best ways to market your business. When you have an event or new product or service, you should announce it. You can post press releases online as well as sending them to the local media outlets. This is something you can do on your own or you can hire a public relations firm to do it for you. Sometimes a Virtual Assistant can handle this as well. Two very afford-able online press release sites are PRWeb.com and PRLeap.com. There are some free sites as well; however, they have limited distribution.

There are many low or no cost ways to market your product or service.

Speaking of announcements, send them out to your contact base whenever you have news. It's a great way to stay in front of people and it shows them you are active, growing, and dynamic. You can also reach out to people in your industry who have blogs and ask them to post something about your news. When you write the copy and provide them with everything you want them to say and show, it is quite easy for them to comply. This is called a '**blog tour**.' You are touring your product through blogs. Most people are happy to help because they know that when they have a need for the same kind of thing, they can call on you.

Crafting a plan that includes a couple of avenues will help you penetrate the market and send your message to those people who should be hearing it.

A word of caution – please don't think that you can only market and still grow your business. Sales is a combination of efforts that include marketing. It also includes prospecting, educating, and proposing. I am breaking it down so you can focus on each area separately. By the end of this book, you should have developed a strategy that includes several methods working in concert with each other.

Throughout the life of your business you should evaluate your marketing efforts for effectiveness. If you find something is not as effective as you had hoped, be prepared to stop and redirect your efforts and dollars to some other method.

Case in Point:

Matt, the print broker, has to market his print services. He has a website that not only describes the different products he offers, but also has a shopping cart so people can buy right from his site. That is one marketing effort.

In addition, Matt has an ad in the local business journal. This magazine goes out to business people throughout Matt's region, so his reach is long with this method. Another method Matt uses is providing coupons to organizations looking for donations for raffles and auctions. When Matt participates in this way at fundraising events he is raising awareness of his business. These organizations always thank the vendors who donate items. Moreover, the person who wins the raffle item is now aware of Matt's business. Matt is careful to only participate in those events where his prospects might be. For example, when organizations hold golf outings they look to local vendors to provide door prizes and goodie bag items. When Matt participates in these events by offering discount coupons, he is marketing to his target market.

Matt has surveyed his potential client base, identified where they are, and established a marketing strategy for getting the message out about his products.

Simple Cents:
If you want to be taken seriously you MUST have an email address where the domain name is not aol, gmail, yahoo, hotmail, etc. Your domain name should be your company name, tag line, or something that directly relates to your business. Registering a domain name is inexpensive and I submit to you a major part of your marketing campaign. You own a business – you ARE a business person. Act like one. Even if you work out of your home. It doesn't matter. You want to present yourself and your business as a professional enterprise if you want people to take you seriously and give you money.

Chapter Three

Prospecting

Who and where are your prospects?

Dick has a car dealership on the edge of town. He sells mid range cars and SUVs. Dick joins the local chamber of commerce. He attends all of the chamber functions and joins the economic development committee. When the chamber has fundraisers he offers discounts on auto services like oil changes and tires. Dick also reaches out to local drivers' training schools and personal insurance agents. He develops relationships with a few people in these fields who become strategic alliances for him.

Dick also creates a blog where he discusses issues relative to the auto industry. He positions a lot of his posts to discuss items relevant to car owners and offers tips and suggestions including how to get the best gas mileage. He offers promotional deals on his blog and has a link to it in all of his literature. He is creating activity and energy around his dealership by engaging people online.

When I had my lemonade stand, I didn't simply rely on the signs and flyers. I went out to my target market and met with people. I used methods to get my information in front of them that made sense for my business. Methods like telling my neighborhood friends when I was having the lemonade stand, telling people I saw on the street – working in their yards or walking their dogs.

Prospecting is about how YOU get in front of people. Once again there are various methods you can use depending on your industry and your comfort level. The most important element of prospecting is this – it is ACTIVE. I say this because I encounter too many people who use passive methods and then wonder why they don't work.

Example of passive prospecting: John opens a tire shop. He wants to get the word out to prospective clients, so he decides to email them. He crafts a message in email format and proceeds to send it out to about 100 people from a list he purchased. Then he waits. And waits. And wonders why no one is coming to his tire shop. Why? Because he didn't prospect actively. He didn't go get them. He put the ball in their court.

There are two problems with this approach. The first is using email as a prospecting tool. Emailing is lazy, non-personal, and ineffective. I submit that people use email to prospect because they want to blanket the field, but aren't considering whether the method is results oriented.

Email has become a major communication method in the past 20 years. Because of that, people are inundated with emails – everyone thinks it's a good way to get in front of people, so everyone is doing it. Think about the emails you receive. How many do you delete without even opening them? How many go into your spam filter?

In addition, you are leaving the sales process in the hands

of your prospect. Their options are: to delete without open-ing, open and then delete, email back, call. What do you think the odds are of someone receiving an email and actually re-sponding to it? Especially when it puts the call to action in the prospect's hands or there is no call to action. Remember the example above - John sent out the emails, but didn't say he'd follow up. He left all of the responsibility in the hands of the prospect. Once again, think about your own experience with receiving emails.

Please note: Email can be an effective way to communicate with someone once you've established a relationship. It just isn't a good way to start a relationship with a prospect.

As I said, prospecting is active. The prospect wants to know that you want to do business with THEM – not just with anyone. This is why it has to be an active process. You have to pursue them and let them see that they matter to you. When your prospecting is passive, you are in essence saying that you'll take anyone as a client; that you really don't care who you do business with. Whoever decides to contact you, that's who you'll take on.

Active prospecting let's people know that they matter; that you've sought them out. Believe me, it matters.

Another thing that needs to be said here is this – you cannot wait for the phone to ring and stay in business. I've had business owners tell me that as long as people seek them out they can bring on new business easily. Howev-er, when they have to go sell, nothing happens. That's be-

Active prospecting let's people know that they matter; that you've sought them out.

cause they are relying on the prospect to do all the work.

As a small business owner, you must sell or you will go out of business. Therefore, you must prospect (it's an integral part of the process). You have to bring people to your business, not just wait for them to show up.

Example: Judy owns a donut shop. She's had a steady flow of customers coming into the shop over the years but would really like to increase her sales. So what does she do? She thinks about some of those clients who buy in bulk for meetings, clients, organizations. She devises a plan to find more people and organizations who could be serving donuts at their meetings and events and she goes to see them – with a sample of her donuts! Now she is actively pursuing new business. She figured out a target market and went after it. By reaching out to people whom she determined to have a need for her product, she is spending her time wisely and increasing her client base. Mission accomplished!

In Chapter One, we defined the value of your product or service and established pricing. From that you can develop an idea of who your target market is. It is those people who need or want your product or service. You can create another target as well – the people who know those prospects. The message will be slightly different. However, it is valuable to prospect to both camps in order to pull in a significant amount of business.

I prefer target marketing because it helps you stay focused. Down the road you can always add another mar-

> **An element of prospecting success is having a specific plan and then working that plan.**

ket segment to your prospecting. However, an element of prospecting success is having a specific plan and then working that plan. It helps to keep things narrow for starters.

One way to select a target market is to look at your current clients. Sort them by revenue and take a look at what you are selling to the high revenue clients. Can you duplicate them? This is called vertical marketing. You market to other companies/individuals in the same industry or area; others who look like your current clients.

Case in Point:

Matt, the print broker, sells to law firms, insurance agencies, car dealerships, and schools for the most part. He has a few miscellaneous customers, but these are his main categories.

Matt has taken a look at what he sells to these industries, how often and in what quantities. He's also looked at the profit margins on each item. From this information, Matt has determined that he should be prospecting to more entities in the top four categories. Because he knows what he sells currently, he knows which items to discuss with prospective clients.

So, Matt creates a list of all of the law firms and insurance agencies in his area. He discovers who the contact person is in each firm based on his knowledge of who he currently works with. From these lists he creates a process for contacting the firms. He says something like, "I specialize in working with law firms, providing them with the printed material they need to effectively run their offices. I have a number of law firms as clients and would like the opportunity to see if I could be helping you out as well."

Because Matt is currently working with law firms, he knows the value he brings to them and can share that with prospective law firms. He does this during his meetings with them. When he proposes his solutions, he is coming from a position of knowledge and strength. His proposals are well reasoned and accurate because of his experience with similar firms.

If you are just starting out, take a look at your value proposition. When you understand why it is of value you should be able to determine who it is valuable to. That leads you to the target as I mentioned. Now, pick a market segment within that target and focus your energies there.

Within a target market, some companies or people will not be a good fit. You discover who those are by knowing what a good fit looks like. What is an ideal client? What makes the best business relationships for you and your product or service? Not sure? Once again, take a look at your current client base. Identify your best or favorite clients. Are there any that don't meet that description? What is it about those two pools? What characteristics make up a good match or a bad one? This is an essential step. You don't want to waste your time – or anyone else's.

An example of this is that your target market is micro-enterprises – very small businesses of 50 or fewer employees. Marketing to medium and large size companies is inappropriate. They do not fit your ideal client profile.

Now, what is the best way for you to get in front of them? There are various methods you can use. We will discuss most of them here. Networking is such a large part of prospecting that it has its own chapter (we'll discuss it then).

As you read about these prospecting methods consider who you are and what you are comfortable with. Successful prospecting depends on selecting methods that you can effectively navigate. If something makes you uncomfortable, please don't do it.

Whenever you are in front of a prospect you are "on." Everything you do and say is scrutinized. If you are uncomfortable with the method you are using, that discomfort will be seen. The danger is that since your prospect doesn't know why you are uncomfortable, they will conclude that you don't believe what you are saying. Your credibility comes immediately into question. You can see the damage that un-easiness can cause.

In addition, if you choose a method you aren't really comfortable with, well, you just won't do it! The discomfort will take over and you will find yourself avoiding prospecting all together. You can't grow your business if you don't prospect. I submit that you can't afford to choose a prospecting method that you will avoid.

As we explore various prospecting methods, consider how they feel to you. Identify the strategies that you will be able to incorporate effectively.

1. Cold Calling

This is the strategy that most people dislike. And, who can blame them? When cold calling, you are reaching out to complete strangers with no idea of whether or not they want to talk to you. The odds of being rejected are high. It is human nature to avoid rejection whenever possible.

This is why most people are ineffective at cold calling. Their distaste for the process is palpable. They don't express themselves effectively so the rejection rate is very high. They then avoid calling. And when they do call, their goal tends to be to get off the phone as quickly as possible – instead of getting an appointment. It's a disaster!

But can it be an effective method? You can increase your odds of landing appointments by doing your research ahead of time. Investigate the companies/individuals you want to speak with. Find out all you can about them. Also, keep the benefits of your product or service on the front burner. Match the prospect's needs with your product. Then, when you call, you have a reason and you have something to talk about.

Having something solid to discuss will help you sound confident and in control. Approach with the value proposition and ask if it's something they'd be interested in discussing further. When they say 'yes', schedule the appointment. Don't try to sell them over the phone.

2. Introductory Information

Some people prefer to send literature as a lead in to calling. I use this approach a lot. The magic is to keep the information short, bulleted, and intriguing. Unfortunately, the reality is that people don't read. You have to capture their attention immediately.

You can use questions that are designed to elicit agreement; for example, "Do you find yourself spending too much time searching for documents?"

Follow the questions with a brief introduction to your company. Always close the letter with a statement telling the prospect that you will follow up with them.

Simple Cents:
Do NOT close the letter with – 'if you find this interesting and would like to discuss further, please call me' – or something like that. Never leave the ball in the prospect's court. YOU have to follow up with THEM.

You can attach a single piece of literature for their review. The point of the letter is two-fold. First you want to acquaint the prospect with you and your company. Second, you want to start a dialogue. You are letting them know that you'll be calling. Then when you do call, you can honestly say that they are expecting your call. See? You've told them you are going to call, so they should be prepared for you to do so. Moreover, you MUST follow up.

Too many salespeople make the initial contact and then never follow up. These salespeople have an expectation that the prospect will contact them, or the salesperson gets busy and forgets to follow up.

These prospecting methods depend greatly on the system you implement. If you are going to send an introductory letter, make sure you schedule a date and time in your calendar for when you will call to follow up.

Simple Cents:
People want to know that you want to do business with THEM. They don't want to feel like you are casting a wide net and will take whatever comes up. It's up to you to show the prospect that their business is important to you. Everyone likes to feel appreciated and important. By taking the time to follow up, you are telling your prospects that you value them. It's so simple and yet can yield huge results.

3. Public Speaking

There are many businesses where public speaking is a great way to prospect. You have the opportunity to get in front of a large number of potential clients and referral sources. You can share your expertise and increase your credibility. In addition, it gives your prospects a good feel for you and your business.

An added benefit of public speaking is that it gives you the chance to be a giver. When you offer a seminar or workshop and invite your contacts you are giving them something without asking for something in return. When you do a good job, the referrals and business will follow.

Simple Cents:
When you create a workshop or speech, do not include self-promotional material. The point isn't to sell your products or services. The point is to share information, educate, enlighten. If you sell during your session you will turn off everyone in the room – the opposite of your goal.

You may have experienced a workshop where the speaker started to share information, and then stopped and told you the details were in his book or DVD. I know I've been to those events. They are never good because there's no depth; you don't learn anything you can use. Frankly, the result is being unhappy with the presenter because they didn't provide what they said they were going to. Learn from their mistake and don't do it.

But, what if you aren't good at public speaking or comfortable with it? Consider gathering experts who are good at speaking and sponsoring workshops or seminars that are of value to your contacts. When you sponsor the event, you get to be in front of those folks and again, are seen as a giver.

4. Newsletter

This is one of those things that could also be considered marketing. It is a vehicle with great potential to share a lot of information with your contacts and prospective clients.

You've heard it said that timing is everything. Well, when you offer a newsletter you are putting yourself in front of your prospects on a continuous basis so that when they have a need, you are top of mind.

The keys to an effective newsletter are these:

- Make sure you can consistently produce one based on the frequency you've decided on (weekly, monthly, etc.)
- Develop a system for gathering the information you will share so it is easy for you
- Keep the information relevant, current, and of value to your readership
- Have someone else proofread it. It is too easy to miss mistakes when you are re-reading your own work. Quality counts!

This is also a place where you can make announcements. Your newsletter readers are a captive audience. If you have an open rate above 20% you are doing really well! Imagine the effectiveness of all those people reading your news. It's a gentle form of prospecting that can yield huge results.

Before you decide to create a newsletter, determine who you are going to send it to and how you are going to increase your subscribers. You'll want to put a sign-up box on your website and blog so when people visit they can sign up for the news-letter.

When you've done a really great job you may find your clients referring you without your prompting. That is really the best of every world!

If you do public speaking you should have a way to ask for subscribers when you speak. I have a little form I use. I put it at everyone's place and before I start my speech I tell them about my newsletter. I let them know that I won't sell their e-mail address or solicit them with it. And they only have to offer their e-mail address – nothing else. This is a great way to increase the list.

5. Referral Based Prospecting

We talk a lot about referrals in the Networking chapter. How-ever, I do want to touch on it here as it pertains to current clients. Asking current clients for referrals works well when it's done effectively.

Once you have delivered on your product or service and have developed a relationship with your client, you are in a position to ask for referrals. The key is knowing which clients will be open to the request. You find this out by developing a solid relationship with them. The better you know them and they know you, the more comfortable you both will be.

When you've done a really great job you may find your

clients referring you without your prompting. That is really the best of every world! There will always be clients who just don't think that way, however. For those, a gentle request can yield great results.

Try this on for size: "Thank you so much for the opportunity to provide you with (your product/service). We really enjoy helping our clients with (whatever the problem is that you solved). If you know of anyone we could help out in the same way, we'd love the chance to work with them."

It's gentle, non-threatening and non-aggressive. There are, of course, other ways to say the same thing. Stay true to yourself and develop a script that you are comfortable with Bear in mind what you don't want to do:

- Ask before you've developed the relationship
- Ask for specific names and numbers
- Push the issue
- Make your client uncomfortable

These same rules apply to asking family and friends for referrals. Use the Golden Rule – if you wouldn't want it asked of you, DON'T ask it of others. Nothing makes a relationship more uncomfortable than asking directly for referrals or money!

The way you build a referral based business with friends and family is to just make sure they know what you are doing and that your business grows best by referral. They will take it from there.

6. Social Media

This is an interesting prospecting tool that is growing every day. Where you go and how you use it are the issues. There are many, many 'networks' out there and you may find that you are invited to join a lot of them.

Be careful that you do not over-commit. Even when

you are invited by people you know, you must ask yourself whether that particular network is one that is of value to you.

Where do you go?

The avenues that seem to be getting the greatest attention these days are LinkedIn, Twitter, and Facebook. Each has its value. YOU have to decide which work best for you.

LinkedIn has value for salespeople in a few ways.

1. You become linked to all of the connections your immediate network is connected to. You can search those people or a topic and ask for an introduction to anyone who meets your criteria. You are, in effect, getting a warm introduction to a potential prospect.

2. You can join groups where you can meet other people who share your interests. You can start discussions and/or comment on discussions and thereby, position yourself as an expert. Bear in mind that you really don't want to be selling here. While some people don't mind it, most people are really looking for people to share information.

3. You can use the 'Q & A' feature to show your expertise and allow others to discover you. You go to 'Answers' and then to 'Answer Questions.' You can drill down to your area of expertise or you can look at the general list. The most effective way of doing this is to set up a system for monitoring these questions so you are ready to answer right away.

Twitter is all about giving. The people who are followed the most are the people who share information. They post links to articles, websites, books, etc that they think other people will see value in. When you do this, you can sprinkle in your own information. Examples of this are posting that you have a new blog post, or posting an event you have coming up. The attraction to Twitter is that you can only use 140 characters. Everyone is limited to getting their point across quickly.

A lot of applications have been created to make Twitter easier to use. These include: **Tweetlater** – for post-dating tweets; **Mr. Tweet** – helping you identify who you should be following based on who you are currently follow-ing and who is following you; and **Tweetdeck** – a utility that sits on your desktop, shows you tweets, replies, and direct messages, and allows you to shorten URLs in your tweets. More are created every day.

Facebook is used by many people for personal commu-nication with friends and family. There are, however, a lot of business people using it for their business. They set up a page that is focused on their business. Believe me, Facebook is not just for teenagers. People of all ages are using it to share information.

The most important thing to remember about social me-dia as a prospecting tool is that you have to be a giver. Indi-viduals who self-promote are left alone – literally.

You should approach Social Media like networking. You are looking for people to build relationships with – either as new clients or referral partners.

Strategic Alliances

Strategic Alliances are reciprocal relationships with vendors in complementary industries who are talking to the same prospect base that you are talking to. Because they are in a complementary industry they are not competing with you and they are hearing the client talk about needing what you have to offer. They can then refer you in – and you can do the same for them.

The salesperson or business owner who creates and nur-tures strategic alliances will see his sales grow. Why strategic alliances? Because they sell your business for you. And, they provide you with additional resources to offer to your clients and prospects. This makes you more valuable to the people you know and meet.

There are three easy steps to creating strategic alliances:

• Think about your target market. Why do they need your product or service? Who are they talking to? Who knows what they need? They're talking to someone. Those are the people you want to ally yourself with. It may be a small business banker, or cpa. Maybe it's their massotherapist. Don't laugh. Most people vent while getting a massage.
• Once you've got some categories, find those people you can build a relationship with. Just because they fit the segment, doesn't mean you're going to click with them.
• Develop the relationship. It's critical that you take the time to develop relationships with your allies. You want to be invested in them, and vice versa. For long term business growth, you need long term relationships.

Case in Point
Matt, the print broker, has done his research and discovers that a good strategic alliance for his business is a company that does vehicle wraps. Vehicle wraps are advertisements on the sides of trucks and cars. You've most likely seen them. These companies call on exactly the same prospective clients that Matt calls on. As a matter of fact, they complement each other so well that they can be direct links between their clients and each other.

Since they are always in front of the same prospects they are always thinking about each other. This is an ideal strategic alliance because it helps both of them.

As you can see there are a variety of prospecting methods you can use. Prospecting is a numbers game. You can't prospect to a small number and expect huge results. Not everyone you come in contact with is going to need and/or want your product or service. So when you are developing your target market, consider how big the pool is. If it's small you need to add in other targets. You may have to tweak the message for a slightly different audience but you need a big audience.

Conventional sales wisdom says you have to be in front of someone seven times to make an impact.

When you consider all of the aspects of prospecting you'll see why it's valuable to select several methods and use them in concert with each other. It's the best way to create energy and impact. The more you are out there, the more people will see you – and the more often they will see you – you will become a known entity.

And remember, as with anything you need a system. Once you've determined the methods you'll use, create a plan of action – how, when, and where you will proceed; what steps you will go through.

Chapter Four

Networking

How do you get You out there?

Harry decided he was going to attend a networking event each week. He explored his area and discovered several networking opportunities. He researched each of them as best he could and then scheduled time to attend.

Harry also devised a plan of action for these events. He established a goal for what he hoped to achieve and built his plan around that goal. With business cards in hand he started attending these events. At each event he met two people. He had meaningful conversations and learned about their businesses. Because he had gotten business cards from each of these people he was able to write them a nice note and mail it out the next day. A few of the people he felt a real connection to so he called them and scheduled a follow up meeting. Harry was now getting himself out there and building relationships.

There's networking and then there's NETWORKING. Some people think networking is going to an event and seeing how many people they can give their card to; or how many cards they can get. Some people think just joining an organization, or just going to the meeting is networking.

I went to a networking luncheon for business owners. There is a period of mingling and networking before the meal and the guest speaker. I watched a woman who had just started her business walk around the room and hand her business card to everyone – yes everyone! – in the room. That is NOT networking. She failed to have a conversation with even one person at the meeting. The result is that no one left the meeting with even an inkling of an idea of who she is or what she does; a truly missed opportunity.

So, what are the aspects of Effective Networking? Let's spend some time on networking events for starters.

Most small business owners I meet are intimidated by networking because they believe they have to meet everyone in the room, hand all of their business cards out, tell everyone about their business, and make some actual connections for future sales.

Well, relax. Nothing could be farther from the truth. Networking is an investment in your business. It takes time and when done correctly can yield great results for years to come.

Event Networking
The first element of Event Networking is FOCUS. Focus on building relationships. You do this by just being yourself and showing genuine interest in others. Go to networking events with the goal of learning something you didn't know before.

Be a giver. When you meet people, really listen to them. If you hear them talk about something they need – even if it's something you don't offer – think about whether you know someone who can help them. If you do, offer the assistance-the introduction.

Remember, people do business with people they know, like and trust. When you are a giver, people are more inclined to trust you. When you aren't trying to sell them, they'll like you. The more you try to get to know them, the more they'll be able to get to know you.

Networking is an investment in your business. It takes time and when done correctly can yield great results for years to come.

Now you are someone they know, like and trust! The added benefit of focusing on building relationships is that it will put you at ease. You will feel more comfortable in the room and that comfort will translate into approachable confidence.

The second element is AP-PROACH. Don't try to sell everyone in the room. And please don't hand your business card to everyone you talk to, or worse yet, everyone in the room.

Remember the story above about the luncheon where a woman walked around the room and put her business cards into everyone's hands? That's a major put-off and unfortunately, not unusual. Don't be one of those people!

Have a plan. Plan to meet and GET TO KNOW one to two people. If the goal is to learn something new and get to know people, you can't possibly do that by blitzing the room. Have a couple of open-ended questions and let the conversation flow. A word of caution here – be present in the moment. Don't be so focused on the next question you want to ask that you miss what the person is saying to you.

When you meet someone who you feel a connection to, suggest getting together for coffee or lunch.

Another critical aspect of Event Networking is FOLLOW UP. This is the step just about everyone misses. And, it's a shame because it is a crucial step. When you spend time talk-ing to someone at a networking event, ask for their card. Re-member – don't give them yours unless they ask for it. That same day or the next, follow up with a handwritten note.

Simple Cents:
DO NOT e-mail the person. Remember, e-mail is informal and lazy. You are trying to build relationships with people who either need your product or service, or know someone who does. Everybody e-mails because it's easy. Well, it's so easy it has no value! You also run the risk that it will get caught in spam and never seen. If the mailing address isn't on the card, call the number or look them up online.

The person you are getting to know may not have a need for your product or service. But, they probably know some-one who does or someone you should be connecting with – a strategic partner. That's the value of effective event network-ing – making connections with people to build long term re-lationships and business success!

The other standard form of networking is Leads Groups. Leads Groups work when all the members understand why they're there.

I belong to a networking group full of really great people. Every once in a while someone joins who doesn't quite get it. They don't come to meetings on a regular basis. They don't meet with the members outside of the group to get to know them. They don't listen when people give their introductions or state their lead needs. And yet, they complain that they aren't getting leads. They have this belief that just because they are in the group they are somehow entitled. Nothing could be further from the truth.

Ultimately, people join leads groups to increase their own business. The METHOD is helping others increase business. If everyone in the group focuses on two things, the group will be tremendously successful.

The first thing is building relationships with the other members. Remember, people do business with people they know, like, and trust. You can't like and trust them until you get to know them.

So, meet them outside of the usual group meeting. Go out for coffee or lunch and start the relationship. Continue to nurture the relationships with the people in the group you feel a connection with. It won't be everyone and that's okay.

A word of caution: don't try to sell those group members at the 'get to know you' coffee.

Example: Barbara joins a networking group. Understanding that the best way to receive referrals is to get to know the people in the group, she schedules coffee with various group members. Nine out of ten of those people try to sell Barbara their products/services at those coffee meetings!

This is NOT the way you work in a leads/networking group. The point is not to try to sell everyone in the room. The point is to build relationships with those people so you have a better understanding of what they do, how they do it, and who their ideal clients are.

Remember, people don't like to be sold, but they do like to buy from people they know, like, and trust. It's hard to get to know someone who is pushing their product on you. Besides, these experiences left Barbara with a bad taste for the group. Those group members destroyed any chance they had of Barbara referring them to her contacts and clients.

The second thing is giving qualified referrals to the other members. It's important to note here that there is the very strong possibility you will be unable to give referrals to every member of the group. There may well be people in the group who offer a product or service that you just can't help with. It's not about one for one, but more like paying it forward.

Focus on quality and value. Give referrals to those people who you can give them to when it makes sense.

So don't worry about equity. Focus on quality and value. Give referrals to those people who you can give them to when it makes sense.

It's also valuable to notice that I've said nothing about focusing on what you can get because that's not how it works. There's a popular saying that you've probably heard – 'givers win.' It's simple and very true.

When you help others solve a problem, you increase your value to them and the people they know. When you connect two people, you are potentially solving both of their problems. The service/product provider or vendor by helping them increase their business and the buyer by helping them get what they need. It's a win-win-win situation.

Now let's talk about referrals. In order for you to give a good, qualified referral you first need to know that the people you might refer are okay with it.

Consider this: Bill tells Ralph that he is targeting CPAs. Ralph says. 'One of my clients is a CPA. Here's his contact info.' So, Bill calls the CPA and leaves a message. A day later Ralph calls Bill and asks how it went with the CPA. Bill explains that he had to leave a message. Then Ralph tells Bill that the CPA called him and asked him not to give his name out anymore.

Now what just happened here? Ralph didn't find out first if the CPA was okay with being referred. Some people just don't want people calling them – even if they could benefit from their product or service. If you want to provide quality leads the best way is to reach out to the person first to make sure they are okay with you giving their name out.

Know your clients well enough to know which ones are open to contacts from others and which ones aren't. The last thing you want to do is jeopardize your relationship with your client by giving his name to someone else if that's not what your client wants.

There are three types of referrals:

1. Cold – these are not really referrals at all and should not be confused as such.
   a. Informational – an article you read, something you heard, the name of a company, or even the name of someone in the company – though you don't know that person so you are no help, really.
   b. This isn't a referral – it's a lead. It's information someone can use to dig deeper. It really doesn't help them get in the door.
   c. These do have value because they tell you more than you knew before, but that's it.
2. Warm – Basically, you've just given the name and possibly the phone number of a contact to a vendor. The vendor can use your name to get in the door. Other than that, you've done nothing to grease the wheels.
3. Hot – These obviously are the best and because of that are fewer.
   a. When you find out someone wants to do business with an organization that you are involved with, you make the initial contact and introduce your vendor friend.
   b. You hear from someone you know that they have a need and you know there is someone in your group who fits the bill. So, you tell your friend/con-

tact about the group member and offer to make the introduction. You let your group member know you referred them, so they can be ready for the call.

Ultimately, what you need to know is that effective networking groups take effort. I've been in a group for 11 years. The core members understand the process and think about each other outside of the meeting. It's not unusual to get a call in the middle of the week from a group member who was talking to someone and found out they have a need for your services. That group member has offered your name and number and has then called you to tell you to make contact. What could be sweeter than that?

Case in Point

Matt, the print broker, belongs to a networking group that meets every other week. Matt brings a small list of companies and organizations he'd like an introduction to. He listens attentively as each member states their lead needs and makes notes where he wants to remember something or get back to someone in the group at a later date. He also carries the business cards of his group members with him so that if he encounters someone with a need he can make the referral.

At the end of the day remember this –how you behave speaks volumes about who you are. Make sure your behavior matches your desired impact.

It's not about how many referrals you give; it's about how qualified those referrals are. Please note – when you give crummy 'referrals' because you want to be seen as giving, everyone sees through it and your reputation suffers.

Example: Betty is in a leads group and says she is targeting Human Resources professionals. Roger passes her a lead, but writes, 'don't use my name', on the sheet. Not only is this not a lead, it's in very poor taste. Roger is letting Betty know that he doesn't understand networking and doesn't know how to refer people.

Not only does this behavior not help the 'lead' recipient, it telegraphs who you are. It tells people you really don't care about them; that you are just trying to appear giving so you'll receive leads. My friends, it just doesn't work that way.

Really committing to the group is key. You have to attend meetings, arrive on time, and be present. There are few things worse than seeing someone walk into a leads group meeting so late that they miss hearing what everyone's lead needs are. Or how about when people talk during this process? Not only is it rude, it sends a clear message that the only person they care about is themselves.

So show up on time and ready to participate. Pay attention to people when they talk and try to be a connector. In addition, be clear and specific with your lead needs. In this way you are helping others help you. The more specific you can be the easier it is for others to land on possible referrals.

At the end of the day remember this –how you behave speaks volumes about who you are. Make sure your behavior matches your desired impact.

There is an added value to networking that needs to be addressed. It is this – when you network you develop a list of resources that you can share with others. This increases your value to those prospects and clients you deal with. Imagine how well you can position yourself with others when they find out that you can help them solve problems that have nothing to do with your product or service.

When people find out that they can call on you to help them solve a problem they will remember you, refer you, and use your product or service whenever they can. That is sales assistance you just can't buy.

Lastly, we need to talk about your elevator speech. This is the 30 second spiel or commercial you will use in your leads group and at networking events. The elements of a great commercial are these:

- Who you are
- What you do
- Who you do it for
- Why it benefits them
- Concise, clear, and value-centered
- Not cutesy

Too many people have a 30 second commercial that goes on for two minutes. At the end the audience still has no idea what the person does or who they do it for. This tool is not for you to say everything little thing you do. It is for you to give a general idea to others about what you do and the value it has for your client.

Case in Point
Matt, the print broker, can print just about anything. However, that's not what should be in his commercial. The overall idea of what he provides to his clients is the central message of his commercial. So it goes something like this:

Hi. My name is Matt and I'm with The Message Specialist. I help companies and organizations of all sizes get their message out through engaging, dynamic, and cost effective print materials.

What does he do? He helps companies get their message out.

Who does he do it for? Companies and organizations of all sizes.

What is the value to them? It is engaging, dynamic and cost effective.

Do you know what Matt does? Exactly! He didn't have to say business cards, brochures, sale sheets, two part forms, etc. He got his point across by carefully wording his commercial.

So when you craft your 30 second commercial keep these points in mind. Remember the 'not cutesy' point? Something creative can be great, but cutesy can be a killer. If you are a realtor and want to say that you are a matchmaker – that is good. If you are a therapist who uses spiritual methodology, don't say something like 'I help people touch their man/woman/child-self.' Huh? Believe me you'll lose people. While that may be what you do, the question to ask yourself is, why is that of value? How does it help the person? Let's say it matters because it helps them let go of past guilt and move forward in a centered, focused way. Then, what you say is that you help people remove the obstacles that are preventing them from living their most productive life. THAT is something they can land on.

.

Chapter Five

Selling

How do you gain clients?

Rosemary has a great selling strategy. When she meets with a prospective client, she thanks them for meeting with her right away. She asks them pre-determined questions about their business. Some of these questions are germane to her product or service. However, many of the questions are designed to help her gain a better understanding of the business and the business owner. Rosemary wants to be sure she really understands what motivates the owner, and what matters to him.

Rosemary takes copious notes and when she feels she's got enough information to go on, she lets the prospect know that she will review the information and put together a solution designed just for them. She ends by letting them know when she'll be back in touch to schedule a time for her presentation.

Rosemary goes back to her office where she reviews the data she's collected and crafts a proposal based on that information. She calls the prospect, schedules a meeting and presents her proposal. At the end of her proposal, she asks the prospect what he thinks and how he'd like to move forward. Rosemary has made her sale!

There are times my thirteen-year old son will come to me with a problem. At first, he believes the problem to be x. However, after we talk for a while, it turns out that the problem is really y. Once clearly identified, we can set about a plan for resolving the issue.

This is how it is with sales. When you meet with a prospect, they may believe their issue is one thing. It is up to you to ask the right questions to make sure you – and the prospect – know what the real issue is. Then, and only then, can you determine if you have a solution.

For our purposes we are going to say that selling begins when you are in front of the prospect. This is your opportunity to tell them about your product or service. The funny thing here is that you want to do less talking – less telling about your product or service.

Successful selling begins with listening. Your job when you are in front of the prospect is to ask questions and then listen to the answers. Take copious notes about what they tell you; what they say and what they don't say.

Your goal is to learn as much as you can about the organization, the needs, the decision making process, the budget, and where applicable, the current vendor. The only way to learn these things is to really listen.

You have to be present when you listen. That means that you can't be thinking about the next question you want to ask. You can't be thinking about how you want to respond to what they are saying. When your mind is over there, you aren't really hearing what they are saying over here.

When you don't listen effectively you lose a lot of the detail. Your ability to respond effectively and match your product to their need is compromised.

So listen well. Come prepared with a lot of questions. It's always easier to think of the questions when you aren't in front of the prospect. So don't free-wheel it. Prepare for the conversation. Whenever you are having a conversation with someone, focus on what that person is saying. Really absorb their words, intonation, and body language. Capture what is truly going on with that person. Discover what is truly important to them. Do not let your biases impact your ability to absorb what they say. People will tell you things that may sound trivial at first; however, how they say it can tell you if it actually matters to them. Sales is about the client, not about you, so listening well is critical. This may take practice. It is well worth the effort.

Sales is about the client, not about you, so listening well is critical.

Case in Point:

Matt, the print broker, meets with a prospective client. He has a list of questions about their print needs including what they are hoping to accomplish with their printed materials. He also wants to know everything they currently print.

Since Matt is the expert, it is part of his responsibility to find out what the prospect is currently doing and match it against what he knows they should or could be doing. It is his job to present them with solutions. First, he has to learn what they are currently doing and how his solution is best there. He has the opportunity to present ideas they are not currently using. He'll have to explain why these things are of value. In other words, why the prospect should consider these new items and not just keep to their old ideas.

In addition, Matt may find that something the prospect is currently doing just isn't getting them the results they desire. It may be because of the current design and format. Or, it could be something they shouldn't be doing at all. Once again, as the expert it is his job to share his thoughts with the prospect. This is one of the ways he shows that he has their best interest in mind and is interested in helping them succeed.

The better you get at listening, the more confidence others will have in you. The more they will believe that you are genuinely interested in their needs, wants, and desires. And, therefore, the more willing they will be to do business with you. You will also be able to determine whether you want to do business with them! You will learn valuable information that may shed light on the intentions, attitudes, and behaviors of the prospect.

If anything makes you feel uncomfortable, go with that feeling. If you are meeting with a prospect and they are telling you things about their business that make you uncomfortable, chances are you shouldn't do business with them. You know when you get that feeling in your gut that there's something wrong? Well, what I am saying here is this – that gut feeling is correct and you should follow it. Your intuition is something that will serve you well in your business if you pay attention to it. Remember that you do not have to do business with everyone! When your gut tells you the prospect across the table is someone you don't want to do business with - walk away.

Make sure you take notes on what you hear. Don't rely on your memory. You want to be able to refer to the specific information the prospect provided when creating your proposal and discussing their needs.

Once you've gathered all of the information, you can respond with a few initial thoughts, solutions, or ideas. Or, you can go away, consider the options, create a proposal and go back for a discussion about how you can help them. Whatever path you take will depend on you, what you are selling, who the prospect is, and the simplicity or complexity of the answer.

This is a critical part of the process. Don't rush through it. Give it the energy it deserves so you maximize the odds of getting the sale.

When you use this process you will accomplish a couple of things. The first is that you will be showing your prospect that they matter to you. People not only like to be listened to – they like to be heard. They want to know that you find it important to discover what they truly need or want. The second thing you'll accomplish is that you'll have a good understanding of what they need. This will give you the ability to really answer their concerns with your product or service. Your solution will be powerful because it will address the prospect's concerns – not what you think they should know. This is where the features come in. You present them as benefits – how they help your prospect based on what he/she said.

A feature is an actual aspect of the product or service. For example, a feature of a dishwasher is the 'china wash' cycle.

A benefit is the value that feature has to the client or user. Using the example of the dishwasher, the benefit is being able to get your delicate items clean without hand washing them.

Remember, it's not about you telling your prospect all the features of your product or service. What matters is that you show the benefit TO THEM that can help solve their problem; the problem you discovered when you asked questions. There is a connection between features and benefits – when you use them the right way.

In addition to the information you gather regarding your prospect's needs, you also need information as the seller. You need to know who the decision maker is, what their budget is, what their timeframe/sense of urgency is in order to be sure you have a clear picture in its entirety. But, what do you do if you can't get all of the information you need from your prospect? What happens if he won't tell you his budget or who the decision makers are?

Example: Ralph starts communication with a new prospect. He asks some qualifying questions but is having trouble getting some hard answers. The prospect won't tell him the budget and isn't clear about who the decision maker is. Ralph has three choices:

a. Keep asking these questions and hoping for an answer.
b. Go ahead and provide a quote based on the other information he's received.
c. Tell the prospect that he really would like to work with them but without these key pieces of information he won't be able to quote accurately and doesn't want to waste their time. In this case, Ralph is ready to walk away from the prospect.

Which avenue do you think is the best one? If you answered 'C', you are right. Ralph chose 'A' and ended up with an angry prospect and no quote. The prospect wasn't going to answer those questions no matter what and got annoyed because Ralph just kept asking them.

If he'd chosen 'B', he would have run the risk of being too high in his quote. Now he could have offered some ranges and let the prospect know that since he didn't have their budget numbers he was offering low, middle, and high solutions. That can work.

I believe 'C' is the best option because when you are talking with someone who doesn't want to provide you with key information you need, they are sending you a signal that either they aren't interested in working with you, or they are going to be difficult throughout the process.

Think about this from your own consumer point of view. When you want information from a vendor, don't you give them as much information as you can so you can get an accurate quote from them? You don't want to leave them to their own devices and run the risk of being quoted a Cadillac solution when what you really want is the Chevy. Or, vice versa.

At the root of all of this is the idea that the salesperson should be managing the sales process – not the prospect. You have to be able to stand firm and be willing to walk away if the prospect isn't forthcoming. Your time is valuable. Use it wisely.

When I spoke with Ralph about his situation, he said that in this economy you want to take every opportunity you get. Okay. My question is this – was this really an opportunity? Maybe he wasn't talking to the decision maker. Maybe the person he was talking to didn't know the budget and therefore couldn't divulge it. Whatever the reason, Ralph wasn't getting what he needed to do his job effectively.

As a salesperson your time is best spent with prospects you can work with. Those are the people who will provide you with the answers to your questions. Your job is to ask those questions and get the answers before you move to the quoting phase. You will be most successful when you are willing to walk away from the people who don't want to provide you with those answers.

You have to be able to stand firm and be willing to walk away if the prospect isn't forthcoming. Your time is valuable.

This leads me to presentations – how you provide your proposal or quote. There really is a right way to do this. When you think about what you hope to accomplish – the sale – your presentation must be created in a way that works toward that goal.

Powerful presentations are structured as follows:

- Short and to the point
- Begin with a recap of the prospect's goals and needs (as you heard them)
- Introduction of the product or service you are presenting
- Bulleted list of the benefits of that product or service to the prospect (based on the goals and needs you heard)
- Cost statement
- Implementation schedule if appropriate
- Request for confirmation from the prospect – ask them how it sounds to them; does it meet their needs as stated.

Notice that the presentation starts with a recap of the prospect's needs and goals. Sales is all about the prospect – not about you or your product/service. When you begin with the prospect's needs/goals you are setting the stage. In effect you are confirming what they told you. Then you are showing the prospect that you heard them when you introduce your product/service and explain the benefits of it. This is followed by what it will cost the prospect. Then, a confirmation statement so you can be sure you've matched your product to their need correctly.

Frankly, when you follow this format you'll get confirmation from the outset. If you are incorrect about the prospect's needs and goals, they'll most likely interrupt you and point that out. If that happens, it's okay. Have that conversation with them by asking them where you are off the mark. And really LISTEN! In this case you'll most likely have to create a new proposal. It's not the end of the world.

What you don't want to do in that situation is continue on with your current proposal because it is irrelevant now.

Responsiveness is critical in the sales process. You may

have an interested prospect, but if you don't get them the information in a timely manner, you run a huge risk. You are telling the prospect that you are unreliable or uninterested in attaining their business. If you can't follow through during the sales process, why would they think you'll follow through once you've got their business?

Example: Debbie works for an office supply company. She meets with a prospective client and finds out which products they use the most as well as their purchasing cycles and practices. During the conversation, the prospects ask Debbie about a new product they've heard about. Debbie is unfamiliar with it, but promises to find out and get back to the prospect with an answer and a proposal. Debbie leaves the meeting and gets on with her day, her week, her month. Debbie fails to respond to the prospect with the product information, and is late in getting them her proposal.

You can imagine how the prospect feels about Debbie! Not only did she fail to get the business, but the prospect is no longer taking her calls or communicating with her in any way. The door has closed on that opportunity. Remember these two things:

1. People talk. That prospect is going to share that experience with his friends and associates. If Debbie ever calls on one of the prospect's contacts, she'll find it hard to get a meeting.

2. There are other companies out there doing exactly what you are doing. Don't make it easier for them to compete against you. How many office supply companies do you think there are in the average city? That's right – a lot. Debbie has a lot of competition. She needs to be on her game at all times or

she is driving her prospects into the arms of her competitors.

Many salespeople tell me that they want ALL of the business in their market. My response is always, "No, you don't." There is no way you do, or should, want all the business out there. Why? Because some of it is really bad business. It's not worth the time or energy you'll give it at any stage of the process.

If you've been in sales for more than a month, you've encountered a difficult prospect. Think about them for a minute. They want a lot for very little. They request more and different information constantly. They are never satisfied, delay decisions, and don't appreciate the value of your product/service. What exactly will you gain by winning that piece of business? You will spend a lot of time on something that isn't profitable. That's time you're taking away from profitable opportunities and current business.

What you do want is all of the good business! A good piece of business is one where you are getting a fair price for delivering a valuable product or service. A bad piece of business is one where you are under-compensated for delivering a valuable product or service.

When you find yourself with a prospect or client who is taking more than they're giving to a significant degree, it is time to walk away. It makes more sense to walk away than to continue in a relationship that isn't a win-win for all concerned. And, while walking away may feel strange, you will gain from doing it. You'll have more time to devote to clients who appreciate and respect what you have to offer. This will also give you the time to do more prospecting to find those good business partners.

There is a flip side to this. When you meet with a prospect for a particular product or service that you provide, don't be narrowly focused. You may miss out on an opportunity to quote on other products.

Example: Helen works for a community college that offers a range of business classes. She gets a call from a prospective client company inquiring about a particular class. She schedules the appointment. At the appointment, Helen is so focused on that one particular class that she doesn't consider whether there are other classes this prospect might be interested in.

Helen doesn't ask enough questions about the company to identify all that they need and connect those needs with her classes. She only focuses on the one need and the class that matches it. She never considered the possibility that since they need one class they may need more. She missed out on an opportunity to go deeper with that prospect. Another school came in and sold the other classes to the client company.

In a case like this, you should always stay with the original reason for the appointment until you've uncovered everything you need to know about it. Then, you should ask more questions to make sure you aren't missing anything important.

Let's spend some time on closing. Most likely you've heard people talk about the value of being a good closer. In my estimation, closing starts at the beginning of the sales process.

I believe that 'closing' is something that happens naturally once you have successfully navigated all of the prior steps in the sales process. Think about it. If you don't prospect well, listen well, problem solve well, and create trust well, there's probably no way you are going to close well.

In essence, if you have a good understanding of the value of your product or service, are successful at identifying your target market and then qualifying prospects within that scope, you should be closing easily. When you look back at the chapters where we discussed these aspects of the sales process, you'll see that by the time you get to the closing stage, if you've done everything else correctly, closing will happen naturally. You'll come to an agreement with your prospect that they are right to do business with you – you are going to resolve their problem; alleviate their pain.

Case in Point

Matt, the print broker, knows that his services are valuable to office managers who need to purchase letterhead, envelopes, and business cards. He's identified companies that are big enough in size that their volumes warrant shopping for the best price point. Matt markets to these companies and when he is in front of the prospects he listens well and takes a lot of notes. Because he knows his industry so well he knows which questions to ask.

Once Matt has gotten all the information he needs he goes back to his office and starts searching for the best printer in terms of price and quality. When he's found the solution that he believes meets all of the prospect's criteria he schedules another meeting with the prospect. At that meeting Matt presents his solution. The prospect agrees that the solution Matt has presented meets all of their needs and they enlist Matt's services. Matt has gained a client and 'closed' the deal easily.

Chapter Six
Objections

When they still aren't buying

Chester has just finished presenting his proposal to his prospective client. He finishes up by asking the prospect what she thinks and how she'd like to proceed. To Chester's dismay the prospect says that she's not sure about the solution and will get back to Chester.

Chester asks the prospect what it is, in particular, that she is unsure of. When she hesitates, Chester starts reviewing with her the information she gave him. One step at a time Chester walks the prospect through the answers to his preliminary questions. About halfway through the process, Chester hits on a discrepancy. The prospect had given him some misinformation. Chester confirms that he now has the correct understanding of the prospects needs and alters his solution to fit. The prospect now feels that Chester's solution is a good one and they sign the deal.

This is the thing that EVERYONE is afraid of! I dare say it is the reason many people do not even attempt sales. I believe that if you learn a couple of things you will not be so concerned with the possibility of getting objections from your prospects.

Objections don't have to be scary. When you work your process effectively and still get an objection, it is an indicator that you either missed something, the prospect didn't tell you everything, or they didn't hear you clearly. Any one of these things can be dealt with easily.

When you know your product, its value, and your pricing, you venture out to prospect for new clients. When you discover those companies/people who need your product or service, you reach out to them. This is the qualifying stage. When done properly you will only be reaching out to those companies/individuals who you believe are really potential clients.

Once you are in front of them you want to have a conversation with them. The goal should be to learn as much as you can about what they need, what they want, and where they are regarding budget. You also must be sure you are talking to the decision maker. This is where you should be listening intently. Remember our conversation about listening? Listen to what is and isn't being said. When you are present and paying attention you will be able to pick up on objection signals.

So, what do you do when you get an objection? Explore it with your prospect. You are missing some vital piece of information. Ask questions to get to the bottom of the real issue. As you delve into the objection, determine whether it's something you can overcome. If it is, explain why this isn't a problem, and then ask the prospect if that resolves their concerns. This is your way of making sure they don't hit you with anything else.

Another option is this – when presented with an objection, ask questions to find out if there are any other issues that need to be addressed. That way you can work on every obstacle.

If the objection is something you can't overcome, let them know. Don't try to work on something that doesn't fit with your company or goals. This is where your clarity works for you. You don't want to compromise your ability to provide outstanding service to them and your current client base. You also don't want to engage in activities that will take you away from growing your company.

Remember, you do not need or want ALL of the business out there. Sometimes it just isn't a good fit. If someone offers objections that you can't overcome, move on.

The goal should be to learn as much as you can about what they need, what they want, and where they are regarding budget.

There is one kind of objection that is sometimes hard to see. If you offer a product or service that requires client input, an objection can be their inability to provide you with the information you need to do your job effectively.

Case in Point:
Matt, the print broker, needs input from his client on the design of business cards. The client should provide ideas of what in the way of graphics, font, and style they are interested in. Matt has a new client who refuses to weigh in. Matt has made several attempts to contact the client regarding the card design but to no avail.

So what does Matt do? This is an objection because it is blocking Matt's ability to work with the client. Matt, at this point, has to decide if this is a client he wants to work with.

If Matt decides to move ahead with the card design he runs some heavy risks.

If the new client doesn't like what Matt comes up with he has just wasted a lot of time working on something that he can't sell. That is time he has taken away from current and future clients.

If the new client goes ahead with the design but isn't thrilled, Matt runs the risk that this new client will speak badly about his services with others. This is negative press that Matt doesn't need.

This kind of situation can be very dangerous for a small business. You can't afford the time that is taken away from revenue generation and you can't afford the possible bad press you'll get. If you find yourself in this situation, deal with it quickly and professionally.

Communicate directly with the client and let them know how much their business means to you. At the same time, let them know that you have an obligation to them to give them the best possible product. This is only possible if they participate in the process. You then let them know that if they are not prepared to participate you will not be able to move forward. Suggest a day and time when you can meet to discuss the possibilities and move the job along.

While you may end up letting them go, they will respect your professionalism and that you didn't compromise your integrity for a piece of business. Believe me, it matters.

Chapter Seven
Account Maintenance

How are you going to keep those clients? How are you going to get more business from them?

Macey owns a photography studio. Her services include personal events photography, family and lifetime portraits, as well as professional photography like headshots, product and corporate event photography. She has a corporate client she works with. Macey photographs all of their products, their workshops, and their C level management staff portraits.

One day, while at the client's site, she overhears her contact talking about his daughter's graduation party. When Macey asks him about it he shares all of the planning and details of the event but never says anything to her about possibly shooting the party. Macey realizes that her client may not know that she does personal photography so she tells him about her experience with similar events over the years. Macey, has now created a greater opportunity for her business with this long standing client.

In this global economy where industries are more and more competitive and commoditized, customer service can be the only thing separating you from your competition.

It's easy to see how much more competitive business is today. And, it doesn't seem to matter what industry you're in. With downsizing, rightsizing, and reorganization at companies around the world, more and more people are choosing to start their own businesses. They're picking franchises or hanging their shingle in the industry they were working in before. It's not just business owners experiencing these challenges. Their salespeople encounter them too.

There isn't much new under the sun. So, what sets them, or you, apart? The level of service you offer. Customer service – good and bad – begins with your attitude toward your clients. Do you like your clients? Do you value them? Those may seem like strange questions, but the way we treat our clients speaks volumes about how we feel about them. A few things are true:

- Without clients you have no business
- It's more cost effective to keep a customer than to seek out new customers
- There are other vendors who offer the same product or service

I can hear you saying 'duh' right now! Yes, those things are obvious. But, let me ask you a question – do you think about them when dealing with your clients? When you do or don't keep in contact with your clients, do these things reverberate in your head? When you have the opportunity to 'overdeliver' do you consider these things?

Example: Tom is a small business owner. He receives a call from a current customer on a Friday afternoon. The customer does a pretty substantial amount of business with Tom.

Now, this client has an emergency need. It doesn't happen often, but they've found themselves in a predicament and need some product by Monday. If Tom decides to help out the client, he will certainly experience some inconvenience – mainly staffing for the weekend. It may even be Tom, the owner, who has to work the extra hours to get the job done.

What should the salesperson do? Should they make it happen or tell the client they can't do it? What would you do? In this case, I can tell you that the business owner decided he didn't want to be inconvenienced and told the client he couldn't help them. If you were the client, what do you think your reaction would be?

You know that saying – what have you done for me lately? It exists for a reason. It's one thing to be there for your clients during normal needs. It's a completely other thing to be there for them when they have extraordinary circumstances. This is where you get the chance to shine; to show them how much they mean to you.

Your clients don't owe you anything and they are not your partner. How you treat them determines whether they'll stick around. I wouldn't be surprised at all if the client mentioned above started looking for another vendor to handle all of their work – not just the emergency needs.

As I said at the beginning, the world is more competitive than ever. What sets you apart is the level of customer service you offer. It translates to how much you care about your clients – how much they mean to you. All other things being equal, customer service may be the only deciding factor. It'll either keep your customers coming back time after time, or send them searching for someone who values them.

Case in Point:
Matt, the print broker, has a client who orders business cards. The client knows that the usual turnaround time is 5-7 busi-

ness days. Four days into the order the client contacts Matt and tells him they have an emergency and need the cards as quickly as possible. Matt contacts the actual printer to find out where the cards are in the production line. Matt then decides to drive to the manufacturer, pickup the cards and hand deliver them to the client, effectively cutting off 3 days in the production cycle. Now THAT'S customer service!

Sales is a tricky business. You have to consistently pursue new opportunities while maintaining the relationships you already have.

Do you think Matt's customer will stay with him after that? Do you think the customer will refer Matt to his friends and associates?

Think about it. Wouldn't you?

Sales is a tricky business. You have to consistently pursue new opportunities while maintaining the relationships you already have.

The greater the emphasis on 'new' the less attention is paid to 'old.' It becomes easy to convince yourself that your current clients are happy; that they're going to stick around; and that you are realizing all the potential business from them that there is. This is better known as the Comfort Zone.

The problems with the Comfort Zone are many. For one thing, you are making an assumption that it's where your client wants to be. That's a dangerous assumption. You don't know at all whether your client is happy with the way things are. Being in the Comfort Zone gives you a false sense of security. You now have no idea what your client believes or what they're doing.

For all you know, they could be shopping for a better

deal. If they aren't shopping, they could be approached by your competitors. How do you know whether they are entertaining those offers? In the Comfort Zone, you don't know.

Moreover, you have no idea if you have all the potential business – because you aren't talking to your client. While you may have secured all of the business in the past – it's the past. Times change, clients change, needs change. If you aren't talking to your client you aren't learning about them – their changes and their needs. While you're in the Comfort Zone, someone else is addressing those issues with your client.

Ask yourself – am I in the Comfort Zone? Be honest with yourself. If you answer yes, it's time to break out of the Zone. Create a plan to sit down with each client and catch up. If you're feeling uncomfortable because it's been a while, bring a small gift like a plant or a book. It'll help ease that awkward feeling. Once you've gotten caught up with your base, set up a system to make sure you keep in touch. Make it part of your routine; put it on your list; mark it on your calendar. Whatever works for you – DO IT!

Once you get out of your Comfort Zone – stay out of it. You'll be a better salesperson. You'll maintain more of your client base while bringing on more business.

I touched briefly on another issue with current clients. Do you have all of the potential business? Many times we win a piece of business and then move on to the next prospect. We don't 'go deep.'

Ask yourself this question – do you have all of the business? If you don't know, you probably don't have it all! By keeping in contact with the client, you can initiate the conversation about what is going on in their world. You can find out the various things they do and need. In your mind you can connect the dots.

Example: Jeff is a printer. He has a client who buys letterhead, envelopes and business cards from him on a pretty regular basis. Jeff is happy with this and has never thought to ask about other printing needs. One day Jeff receives a calendar in the mail from that client. Guess what? That's a printing need that Jeff knew nothing about so he missed out on that piece of business.

Don't assume that your client knows all of your products and services, and would contact you. It's your job to keep in touch with them – not the other way around.

Create a system to continue to be in front of your clients learning about their needs.

Chapter Eight
They Buy You First

Always put your best foot forward

Sally is a management consultant. She works with the leadership of mid-size companies, helping them structure their departments to be more productive. Sally meets with prospective clients at their offices and always looks and acts professional.

Sally belongs to a rather large networking organization that has numerous events throughout the month. When she attends the evening events she is usually in very casual clothes, doesn't carry her business cards, and monopolizes the conversation.

One day it occurs to her that she isn't getting any real traction from these events; no one is referring her and very few people are seeking her out to get to know her better. She has failed to remember the cardinal rule – You are always a representative of your business, so be sure you act like one at all times. Sally has painted her business into a corner where there is no new business coming her way.

As a small business owner or salesperson you are always on. You are always presenting, marketing, selling and producing. Failure to acknowledge this will prevent you from being as successful as you could be. I dare say it can actually do harm to your business.

Let's break it down and take a look at each area.

1. Presenting

No matter where you go or who you connect with, you are always a representation of your business. How you speak, what you say, and how you conduct yourself telegraphs volumes about your business to others.

Consider how you want others to view your business before you go out into the world. The walls really do have eyes and people really do pay attention. Don't think for a minute that you can share dirty laundry or gossip with the people you interact with. Well, actually you can do it; it just isn't a good idea. You'll leave them wondering what you say about them when they aren't around.

If you have a difficult client, fire them. Don't complain about it to others. You are a professional. Handle it!

2. Marketing and Selling

These two go together and are sometimes hard to separate. Marketing and selling are information giving activities. However you share information about your product or service, you are marketing and selling. Keep that in mind as you go about your daily activities.

Let's talk for a minute about business cards. They are a marvelous, inexpensive marketing tool when used properly.

The other day, I was meeting with a client at a local coffee shop. A man walked in who she knew and they started talking about work. As he talked about his shop my client mentioned how she refers people to those kinds of stores often and asked him for his business card.

He didn't have any on him. My client commented that I would tell him he should always have his cards on him. SHE learns well! Anyway, his comment was that cards just end up in the circular file.

This man is operating under some common myths. Myths I'd like to dispel here.

The first myth:

The 10 to 15 cents you pay for the card is worth more than the potential business you are missing by not having them on hand. Business cards have value because they take you with the person you give it to. They are reminders. And if you've got them, use them. What good are they doing you in the box on your desk?

The second myth:

When you have business cards you are supposed to hand them out to everyone you meet or run into. Not so. You carry your cards with you so that when someone ASKS for it you can give it to them. This eliminates the possibility of the recipient throwing away the card. They want to have it!

Consider the story above. My client wanted the man's card so she could refer him to other people. There's nothing better in sales than a warm referral. She asked for them because she wanted to use them. She wasn't being polite. She wasn't going to throw them away.

The man in this story doesn't see the real value of

Consider how you want others to view your business before you go out into the world.

having business cards. He isn't using them as the marketing tool they are meant to be. I can say the same thing for sale sheets, brochures, slicks. Any marketing material you have is only as good as how you use it.

The last marketing topic I'd like to touch on here is website usage. So many businesses either don't have a website or don't have their e-mail attached to it. Your website is one of your most valuable marketing tools. It's on 24-7-365. You can drive people to it. You can highlight any and every thing about your business. When your e-mail address is attached to it people are reminded of your company every time they send you an e-mail – or get one from you.

Too many small business owners have their e-mail address at Yahoo!, g-mail, hotmail, or aol. The message they are conveying is that they really aren't serious business people. It's unprofessional and can be damaging to your reputation and success.

3. Producing

The most interesting thing about producing is that it plays an integral role in marketing and selling. After all, how well you produce tells others whether they should buy what you're selling. Producing is a sales tool.

No matter who your clients are, and no matter what they are paying you, you must produce to your utmost ability all the time.

If you decide to do some pro bono work, or discount your rates for a friend, it doesn't mean you can discount the product or service that you deliver. When you make the choice to discount your rates, you are saying that you plan on producing at the same top level for less money. YOUR CHOICE!

Here's an example:

A business consultant decides to offer his services to his friend at a discount. Unfortunately, he provides that friend, who is now a client, less than his usual level of consulting. He doesn't follow up. He doesn't set the same meetings he would set with a client paying full price.

His friend/client is left feeling underserved. That same friend has been referring this person because they are friends and she believes in him. So he HAS been gaining more than payment from his friend. He isn't, however, providing a high level of service to his friend. The result is that his friend, who isn't receiving what she expected from the consultant, is unhappy. She's feeling that she is spending money without receiving the service. And she's feeling that her friend is taking advantage of her. Well, in reality, he is.

You see it was the consultant's decision to discount his prices. If he had planned on providing lesser services he should have told his friend so she could have made an informed decision.

The lesson here is this: Always provide outstanding service. Under-promise and over-deliver. Don't discount your prices if you aren't prepared to provide outstanding service.

Remember, you are always on. People are always drawing conclusions about your product or service based on your behavior. So, make the decision that you are in business to stay; to succeed. Make the decision that you are going to present yourself and your business in the best possible light. Don't let YOUR behavior negatively impact your business.

> **The lesson here is this: Always provide outstanding service. Under-promise and over-deliver.**

Case in Point:

Matt, the print broker, is always dressed for business. Although he works out of his home he never knows when he will be in front of prospects and clients. So he dresses for work every day.

He also has his business cards on him wherever he goes. When he is out at a client's site or at a networking event his listening ears are on. Matt pays attention to the people around him and behaves with courtesy and curiosity. He is always aware of how he is presenting himself to others. Matt knows that a potential client or referral could be sitting right in front of him – no matter where he is.

So, unless he is at home with the doors closed and the shades pulled, Matt is on.

Chapter Nine

Planning To Grow

Growth doesn't happen by accident.

It is the first day of the month and George is in his office making plans. He has reviewed the previous month's production and revenues, as well as his sales figures and pipeline.

Based on this information, George sets up his goals for the coming month. But he doesn't stop there. He works backwards to devise a plan for achieving those goals. Taking all things into consideration, George plans his activity for the weeks to come. He now has measurable steps to take in pursuit of his success.

Goal setting is tremendously important in business. As business people we set goals throughout the year – where we want to go, what we want to accomplish, growth we want to experience. In other words, to attain success as we define it.

The key to reaching those goals is planning. If you want to reach your goals, you have to plan the steps you need to take to get there. Sounds simple, right? And it should be. However, this is the area most people ignore. They set their goals, and then get to the business of each day, never planning the process for reaching those goals. In the end, they may or may not reach their destination. They've left it to chance.

If you are going to take the time and energy to set goals, give them the attention they deserve. Set yourself up for success for reaching your goals. Steps to follow to reach your goals:

1. Once you have the goal, work backwards establishing the steps necessary to achieve the goal
2. Be specific regarding the steps you'll take to reach your goal
3. Follow those steps exactly
4. Be prepared to make adjustments to your planning where necessary
5. Visit your goals and your plan on a daily basis
6. Monitor your progress on a weekly and quarterly basis
7. Enlist the help and encouragement of others where appropriate

These steps seem basic. As Jim Rohn, the internationally known business expert says, "Success is neither magical nor mysterious. Success is the natural consequence of consistently applying the basic fundamentals." The basic fundamentals are having a plan and working that plan.

When you are new to a process like sales, planning becomes even more important. You have to set up the system you are going to use, understanding the results you hope to achieve. As you work that plan and monitor its effectiveness you can make changes if you need to.

> '*Success is neither magical nor mysterious. Success is the natural consequence of consistently applying the basic fundamentals.*'
> **Jim Rohn**

You will also be able to see and own your results. This is powerful because it will motivate you to continue. Results are, ultimately, what matter. So, before you embark on your sales strategy, decide what you want to achieve. Know what your goals are and working backward, establish the system for getting there. That system is made up of the elements discussed in previous chapters of this book.

As you proceed, keep an eye on the effectiveness of your plan. If it needs adjusting – do it. Don't be so set in the plan that you follow it to extinction. As you grow your needs will change. It's not uncommon for your plan to require alterations to match that growth.

Case in Point:
Matt, the print broker, sets out a sales plan at the beginning of each year. He has his goals and his action plan. At the beginning of each week, Matt plans his days ahead.

And then, at the end of each week, Matt reviews his performance. He pays attention to what worked and what didn't. If something didn't go according to plan, Matt investigates to find out why. Maybe it was the wrong activity; maybe it was the wrong timing; maybe Matt got in his own way. Whatever the cause, Matt makes adjustments for the week ahead.

At the end of each quarter, Matt runs reports to see where he stands in relation to his yearly goals. In this way, Matt can make adjustments as he goes along instead of finding out at the end of the year that he didn't hit his goals. This method works well for Matt and ensures that he will be able to hit his targets year after year.

Getting Stuck

If you notice that you've stopped growing, consider that you may be stuck. The longer you do something, the better you get at it. True? Sure. However, there is also the possibility that you stop growing and get stuck where you are, unable to see alternatives or opportunities. I call this being stuck in your view. You get so entrenched that you can't see out.

This is a situation where you've done all the right things to get to a profitable, stable place. Your sales are good, and your relationships with clients and prospects are going well. You feel you have a system that works for you. So you keep doing it – doing the same things over and over.

Not a bad plan unless you find yourself experiencing one of these warning signs:

1. Your business has been at a plateau for a while – for a year or more. It may even be slipping a bit
2. You're satisfied but not hungry
3. You aren't energized to jump out of bed and hit the ground running
4. You find yourself engaged in a lot of detail work instead of a lot of prospecting and relationship building

What's really happening is that you are getting stale; like day old bread. Your world has become so routine you've actually stopped growing. You aren't exploring anymore. It's just not fun, is it? You are in your way. If you aren't motivated to acquire more business with enthusiasm and you lose clients through natural attrition, you are going to find your business heading for a downward spiral (the wrong direction). The longer it takes you to realize your situation, the harder it's going to be to change it.

So, what do you do to spice things up and jumpstart your energy for growing your business? The goal is to keep what works and change what doesn't. To do that, you first have to identify those things. Change your view - step back and take a critical look at how you conduct yourself on a day-to-day basis. Also, put down on paper the process you currently use. Highlight the parts that you enjoy most. Now take a good, hard look at that process. Ask yourself if it's really still working for you or if some changes should be made.

Solicit the help of others. Talk to other salespeople or small business owners. Ask them what process they use to acquire new clients. You might also want to ask them what they do to keep things interesting and fun. Once again, you are looking at things from a different view – someone else's. Enlist the services of a business coach. Most coaches are adept at looking at situations from various angles and helping their clients explore alternatives.

Ask people who know you well how they see you. You can ask them what they think makes you good at what you do, or you can ask them what they see as your strengths. You may hear things you never thought of. The people we know see us through their own window so their view is always going to be different from ours. This can be a life-changing experience!

Feel free to adopt ideas that work for others if they sound good to you. However, don't try to incorporate a system that feels uncomfortable simply because you are looking for a change. That won't work.

I find that when people are 'stuck in their view' it takes

them a while to truly own it. Once they accept where they are, they are in a position to affect change. You owe it to yourself to create your best view. Begin by accepting the idea that you are allowed (and really required) to change your view from time to time to keep it interesting.

Action cures a lot of things – fear, anxiety, inertia, etc. So give yourself a nudge, a push – however slight. Move to a different window, or walk out a different door and take a look. What do you see?

Wins and losses

Part of the planning process is learning from your successes and your failures. The one thing I consistently say to my clients is "I can only live in reality. Won't you join me here?" The point is that you owe it to yourself to know how you are really doing.

Having goals is essential to growth. So is evaluating your progress. When you win, celebrate. And then take a look at how you got to that win. What steps did you implement? How did the plan come together to get you that success? When you lose, own it. Don't beat yourself up but rather, learn from it. What steps did you implement, or not? What happened along the way that created that result?

> **Action cures a lot of things – fear, anxiety, inertia, etc. So give yourself a nudge, a push – however slight.**

This is invaluable information that will only help propel you forward. Be honest with yourself. When you can take a stark, honest, realistic look at the impact your actions and decisions are having on your business growth you will be miles ahead.

Monitor You

When you have a business goal you can use it as a measuring stick for your actions and decisions.

Example: Mary is a graphic designer. She has a partner in the business and they share the sales effort. They set a goal to increase revenue by 15% while maintaining their current client base. As they set out to reach that goal, Mary sits her partner, Ralph, down and tells him that she has a sales strategy that she wants him to use. Ralph thanks her but says he has his own methodology and is comfortable. Mary doesn't let go. She insists that Ralph use her system.

Now what is Mary's goal? It is no longer to increase revenue by 15% while maintaining their current client base. Her goal has shifted to having things done her way.

If she had asked herself how her decision to approach Ralph was in keeping with her overall goal, she may have thought that she had the best way of reaching that goal. However, when Ralph said he had his own method that he was comfortable with, she should have left it alone. When Ralph and Mary follow the path that is right for each of them, the goal will be attained.

Mary should have believed that Ralph was working toward the goal just as she was. The better goal focused decision would have been for each of them to follow their own paths and maintain awareness of how those paths were working out. Then, if something wasn't working right – it wasn't getting them to their goal – they could then revisit their methods and adjust.

Monitor your Environment

One of the things you have to stay on top of is what is going on in your area. What's the economic state? What are the buying habits of the consumers and companies around you?

As I write this book the economy is in some turmoil. Some industries are hurting, scaling back. Some companies are going out of business or hunkering down to try to weather the economic storm.

You must be aware of these things because they impact how you sell, what you sell and who you sell to. You may find that you have to expand your target market to include industries you hadn't thought of before. There are many manufacturing firms considering newer industries to pursue like alternative energy industries because their traditional client base is dwindling.

At the same time being aware of the landscape may tell you to stop prospecting to a particular client base. Knowing which industries and individual companies are having trouble will help you adjust your sales strategy to remove those uncertain firms and add in newer, more stable companies.

Some companies are adding new products or adjusting their current products to meet the needs of new markets. It may not take a lot of effort or expense to make a modification to one of your products in order to make it attractive to a new target market.

Follow up

Throughout this book I've touched on follow up here and there. It is so critical to successful sales that I want to really address it here. No matter which aspect of the sales process you find yourself in, there is an opportunity for follow up.

Many people tell me they just don't have time to follow up. I submit they don't have time not to follow up! The key to successful follow up is developing a tracking system. Decide what methods you want to use for touching the contact. This depends on results and desired outcomes. In other words, pick a method and then monitor it for effectiveness. If you find it isn't working for you, change it. Whatever you do, don't abandon the idea of follow up!

Follow up in the Sales Process

When you are selling, your follow up can be the difference between getting the sale or not. Think about it – what is the point of making the initial contact (cold call or introductory letter) if you aren't going to follow up with a phone call? Why bother? Do you really think the prospect is going to call you? Sometimes they do. More often than not they don't. You're the salesperson. It's up to you to show the prospect that their business is important to you. There are several ways you can stay in contact with prospects: calling, sending snippets of information you think might be of interest to them, and sometimes e-mailing. Please note that e-mailing can be used here when you know the person you are trying reach is often out of the office or uses e-mail more than any other communication vehicle. Establish a program and stick to it. Like any habit, it gets easier once fully adopted.

Follow up with New Acquaintances

When you meet someone at a networking event, luncheon, seminar, etc., ask them for their business card and follow up with them. Sometimes just a handwritten note is sufficient. Depending on who they are and the conversation you had with them, you might want to drop them a note and suggest a future meeting. Once again, you'll have to follow up on the suggestion. Don't wait for them to call you up. They might, but if it's important to you to develop a relationship with them – prove it. Call them.

Follow up with Old Acquaintances

Have you ever run into someone you knew in the past, but for some reason you had lost contact with them? Whether they are someone you want to establish a current relationship with or not, send them a handwritten note telling them how nice it was to see them. If you have no interest in pursuing a relationship, wish them well. If you do want to keep in touch, suggest a meeting. And again, follow up on the suggestion.

Follow up with Clients

Some people are in constant contact with their clients so follow up may seem unnecessary. I submit that everyone should be following up with their clients on a regular basis. This can take the form of a survey, a drop-in, a note thanking them for their continued business and support, a small gift, and so on. Choose one or more methods depending on your client base, and establish the routine to make sure it happens.

Follow up on Referrals

One of the worst things a salesperson can do is fail to follow up on a referral. That failure speaks volumes about that salesperson – their disorganization, lack of attention to detail, disinterest in growing their business, acting unprofessionally. It can also do damage to your relationship with the referrer.

Example: Jessica sells coffee services to companies with five or more employees. One day Henry contacts Jessica and tells her about a client he has who is interested in talking with her. But Jessica never gets around to calling on that referral. Now Henry's client is left to wonder about his judgment and Jessica looks unprofessional. There is nothing good about this scenario. The future affect is huge. Henry will most likely refrain from referring Jessica again because he can't count on her to follow through.

In addition, when someone gives you a referral – and you pursue it – follow up with the referrer. Thank them and let them know how it turned out. Showing your appreciation will let them know that you value them as a networking partner.

If someone gives you a referral and you are in a position where you can't take it – tell them right then. Better to be honest than to take it and not pursue it.

Overall, remember this – finish what you start. If you are going to take the time and energy to participate in the sales process, follow it through all the way. Anything else is fool-hardy.

Fear of follow up

A subscriber to my newsletter contacted me after he read my article on Follow Up. He told me that he struggles with follow up because this is the place where he might experience rejection.

Yes, that possibility exists and can be the reason you don't follow up effectively if at all. However, I submit you can, and should, look at it a different way. The other person isn't rejecting you; they don't know you. It has nothing to do with you! They simply think they have no need for your product or service. So what?

There are plenty of people who will have a need for your product or service. You'll never find them if you don't follow up!

When I went into sales, my father (an expert salesman) told me that it takes ten no's to get a yes. So, he said, when someone says no, thank them with a smile in your voice and move on. You are now that much closer to a yes.

To this advice I will add my own. Get your ego out of it. It's not about you. It IS about them – their needs, desires, goals, viewpoint, belief system. You miss out on golden opportunities when you allow fear to keep you from following up. You are also sending the message to those potential clients that you don't want to do business with them. Isn't that contrary to your real goals?

Chapter Ten
It's All Relative

Relationships make the world go 'round.

Aaron is passionate about his bicycle renovation shop. He loves every aspect of the business. From finding the used bikes to recreating a mode of transportation that stands the test of time, Aaron can't wait to go to the shop everyday.

In addition, Aaron loves his customers. From the very young to the very old, he enjoys working with each person to create the perfect bike. He also has a system for keeping in touch with his customers. He wants to know how the bikes are holding up and how his customers are enjoying their new ride.

Aaron enjoys a huge referral business-most likely because of his attitude toward his work and his clients. The people who are referred to Aaron have an expectation that they are going to have a great experience. And, they do!

Aaron has figured out that it's the relationships that matter most to his business.

There is an overriding topic throughout this book, and it is that sales is about relationships. It's about the relationship you have with your company, your clients, your prospects, and your network.

Your Company

How you feel about your product or service is critically important to how successful you'll be trying to sell it. People can see discomfort a mile away. Remember I said that you have to see the value of your product or service before anyone else will.

You have to believe that you have something that others need or want. YOU must see the value in it. This is the beginning of the success (or failure) of your business. This may sound harsh, but if you went into business for yourself simply because you didn't want to work for someone else anymore, I submit that is an insufficient reason.

You have to have a passion for your business. It takes work to make a business successful. I can't imagine putting that much energy into something you aren't passionate about.

In addition, it is from that passion that you find your creativity when it comes to marketing and prospecting. It's that passion that commits you to creating a sales process and then working that process every day.

It is time for a gut check. How passionate are you? How committed to your success are you? That is the start, my friend.

Your Clients

You may be thinking that it's obvious that you would have a relationship with your clients. What I'm suggesting here is that you reconsider that relationship. Ask yourself how deep those relationships are.

Throughout your company's lifetime you should evaluate these relationships. If you come upon some that aren't quite what you had in mind, it might be time to let them go. If you find you have some relationships that are in their infancy, this is a signal to get closer. Start paying attention to those clients.

You want to be sure you are meeting all of their needs where you can. The only way to do this is to be connected to them. And remember, sometimes the way you help them is to help them solve a problem unrelated to your business. When you position yourself as their partner you become an integral part of their business. That's a great place to be.

A word of caution here is this – remember that they are not your partner. They don't have to be understanding of the things that challenge you. As long as they are paying you they have the right to expect outstanding service all the time.

If, when you review your client relationships, you find some that you think you've neglected, chances are they feel neglected. You are leaving yourself open to being replaced. All it takes is someone else to come along and pay attention to them.

Remember I said that the client wants to know that you value their business? Here is where that plays in. If you are neglecting them and someone else comes along who appears to care about them, they will leave you. They believe that you don't care whether they stay or go. So they are going to go where they feel appreciated.

How you build relationships with your prospects will determine which prospects become clients.

Your Prospects

How you build relationships with your prospects will determine which prospects become clients. This process is like dating. When you start dating someone you take care to communicate effectively. You listen and are attentive. You work to create the best possible relationship. You're honest and have the other person's best interest in mind. See the similarity?

This is true for prospects as well. You have to have their best interest in mind. Remember, they want to know you care about them. They don't care about what you need or want to sell. They just want their needs met.

So, whenever you are with a prospect, pay attention. Really listen to them. Respond to their needs with either a solution or the honesty that you can't help them.

People will spread bad news at a much faster pace than good. news.

Even if you can't do business with a particular prospect you still want to be professional and helpful. This is still a relationship that could serve you in the future. If you think that anyone can be a good referral source for you, you'll realize that you should be treating everyone well. A lost prospect can still refer you to their associates and contacts if they like the way you do business.

There's something called a 'negative referral.' This is where a person shares negative things about you or your business. You need to know that whenever you are out and about, meeting people and dealing with clients and prospects there is the possibility of generating these 'negative referrals.' People will spread bad news at a much faster pace than good news.

This is one of the reasons that you have to use caution when dealing with prospects. You should be on your game at all times with prospects. When I say that I don't just mean being professional and respectful. I mean paying very close attention and determining whether you should be working with that company or not. Pursuing a potentially bad prospect can do real damage to your reputation and your business.

Consider this: You start the dance with a prospect. They are not very forthcoming with information but you think you really want to do business with them. So you keep meeting with them, trying to find different ways to get the information you need. They, on the other hand, demand information from you without any guidelines. If you decide to quote you run the risk of being way off base. If they feel like they've played you, your reputation has taken a ding. You are considered less worthy – a sense they may share with their contact base.

When you work from integrity and hold firm to your beliefs – those beliefs that tell you how a client relationship works best for you and the client – you will walk away from the prospect respectfully and professionally. There is now no wind in their sails. There is nothing bad for them to say, and your reputation will remain intact.

In the case of working with a prospect that IS a good fit, you always have to be on top of the process. Pay attention to everything. Provide information in a timely fashion. Manage the process effectively. The business will be yours to get, or lose.

Your Network
This includes the people in your leads group, your friends, family, associates, contacts – everyone in your circle. How you handle these relationships can make the sales process easier or harder.

If you always proceed with the idea that you aren't going to treat anyone in a way you wouldn't want to be treated, you will be ahead of the game. This can be as simple as acknowledging an e-mail even if you think it doesn't require a response. If someone refers you, send them a thank you note.

Consider how you can help others. Keep them in your thoughts as you travel along. One of the best ways to build loyalty is to be a connector. Another way is to share information. When you come across a good event, article, group, or person, share it with those people who you think could benefit from it.

When you are seen as a giver, others will want to help you succeed. When you are a genuine, honest person who operates with integrity, others will want to share your space. They'll want you to be successful because you are one of the good guys.

Now here's the question – are you asking yourself what this has to do with sales? The answer is; everything! Successful salespeople are great relationship builders. And they build real relationships – they don't fake it. Quite honestly, you can't fake it. People are too smart and see right through any fake attempts at relationship building. Have you ever met someone in a networking environment who tried to make you believe that they wanted to build a relationship with you when all they really wanted was to sell you something? You noticed that, didn't you? That's what I'm talking about. Everyone notices when people are giving lip service to relationship building. So be sincere.

The more good relationships you build in every area of your business, the more successful you will be. You will be presented with more opportunities to sell than you would be on your own. So, when you think about it, one of your marketing and prospecting methods should be building as many good relationships as you can.

I can tell you that no matter where I go or who I meet, I always try to add value to others. Whether it's in person or online networking, I try to connect others and share information. I gather information because I've found that I can then share it with others. People know me as a solution provider. People reach out to me for guidance, information, education, and referrals. Wherever I can, I accommodate WITHOUT EXPECTING SOMETHING IN RETURN.

That is a key statement. I don't think about what it is going to get me. I think about how I can help. Because of that, I am rewarded time and again. If you learn nothing else from this book, please learn this.

Case in Point:
Matt, the print broker, is very aware of the business relationships he has. He touches base with his clients on a regular basis and is always watching out for news or items that may be of interest to them.

When it comes to prospects, Matt stays in consistent contact with them. Because he listens well, he is always able to initiate a conversation and move the process along. Matt's integrity and honesty serve him well with new prospects (as well as everyone in his contact base).

Because of these attributes and his level of expertise, Matt has established a remarkable contact base. There are people throughout Matt's world who know him, trust him, and refer him on a regular basis. Matt makes sure that he lets them know how much he appreciates them and always looks for ways to help them grow their businesses.

Chapter Eleven

Review

What it's all about

We've covered a lot of information here and I trust you are developing an idea of how you should proceed with your sales process. Let's review the highlights:

1. Believe in your product or service
2. Identify the actual value it brings to your clients
3. Have clarity about what it is – what it looks like
4. Determine accurate pricing
5. Select the prospecting methods that work well for you and your industry
6. Networking is key to sales success
7. When you are in front of a prospect, sell by listening
8. Have comfort with the closing process
9. Don't fear objections
10. Stay connected to your clients
11. Present yourself well, always
12. Create your strategy, work it daily and monitor it consistently
13. Celebrate your wins and investigate your losses
14. Successful sales is about building relationships

Believe

You decided to start a business because you believed you had something valuable to offer. Maintaining that belief will help you in the sales process. It is that belief that will keep you working your strategy day after day. Just remember the value your product or service brings to others. This is your opportunity to help those people, alleviate their pain, help them solve a problem. That's what you wanted to do, isn't it? Think of it as a football game – it is a game of inches; you just have to keep moving the ball down the field.

Value

From that belief you can identify the value your product or service provides to your clients. Knowing value is imperative. Your marketing message will speak to that value.

Clarity

Be clear about what it is you offer. The more specific the easier it will be for you and your prospects to land on it. It also makes it easier for you to price it and speak about it. Your marketing message will be clear, and your conversation with prospective clients will be clear.

Accurate Pricing

How you price your product/service is a key element of your sales and marketing process. If you price too high you'll have difficulty selling its return on investment for your clients. If your price is too low, you undervalue your product/service. You may find that you can't sustain your business even if you have clients.

Prospecting

There are different methods that, when used in concert, can yield great results. The key is to figure out which methods work best for you and your business. Implement them and then monitor them to be sure they are working for you.

Networking
Meeting people who you can build relationships with will help you grow your business. Attending networking events and joining leads groups are essential to the sales process. It is a process that takes time to build.

Selling
No one likes to be sold. People do, however, like to learn. Selling is about listening and then sharing information that is relevant to what you've heard. Listen, take note of what you hear, and then respond with a solution to what you've heard if indeed you have one.

Closing
The best way to be comfortable with the closing process is to master the prospecting and sales process. When you follow the strategy you've selected, and that strategy works, you will find that closing is a natural extension of that process.

Another way to look at it is this – when the fit is there, the prospect will want to buy.

Stay Strong
Objections are simply miscommunications or misunder-standings. They actually help you navigate the process. If you encounter an objection, have the conversation; ask the questions you need to ask to discover what the real problem is. If you can overcome it, great. If you can't, move on.

Stay Connected
Once you've navigated the process and have secured the

business, your job is not done. An integral part of sales is account maintenance and penetration. You want to keep the business you worked to get. You also want to work on gaining all of the potential business there is.

Present Yourself Well

People are always paying attention and developing their opinions about you and your business. How you present yourself helps them draw those conclusions. Make the decision to always present yourself in the best possible light. It will serve your business well.

Strategize

You can't sell effectively by leaving it to chance. You have to determine the plan you want to execute and then put it into action. At the same time you should be monitoring your progress. Keep an eye on how your plan is working for you, and make adjustments where necessary.

Relationships Matter

Business is between people. How you develop and nurture relationships will play a major role in how successful you are at selling your product or service. Build good relationships with people who you feel a connection to.

Celebrate and Investigate

The way we improve our performance is by taking a realistic look at our results. When you gain a sale, celebrate! When you lose a sale you thought you should have, investigate what happened. Learn from the experience. If you can look at it realistically and adjust your process, you can achieve better results.

You have to be open to growing as a person and a salesperson in order to continue to grow your business. The world is ever changing. New prospecting methods are created, clients change, environments change, new prospects appear, and your company will change. Staying alert and aware of these changes, as well as being open to change, will help you grow your business.

Glossary

Authentic – Just be you! I use this word to describe the you who you are. Successful salespeople operate from a position of authenticity. They are being themselves and staying true to their values, beliefs and ideals.

Call to Action – This is the step you are going to take to draw the prospect in; to obtain the opportunity to have a conversation with them. When you are approaching a prospect with marketing material or an introductory letter or phone call, you don't want to put the 'call to action' in their hands. You want to let them know what your call to action is going to be. In the case of a phone conversation you want to take the call to action and request a follow up conversation or action on your part.

Closing – This is the actual point at which the prospect buys your product or service. It is the final step of the sales strategy

Cold Calling – This is exactly as it sounds. It is calling people you do not know, have never met, and have no idea if they need your product or service. You are calling them to begin a dialogue about how you may be able to help them

Negative Referrals – This is when someone spreads bad news about you or your business. It has the opposite effect of what we know of as referrals. Not only will those who hear the negative not do business with you, they will most likely continue to spread the bad opinion.

Networking – meeting people in various industries and venues who may need what you have to sell or may know someone who does. You might also meet people who become good resources for you; people who can help your clients and contacts.

Objections – these are the reasons people don't buy. It's the resistance you feel when you are making your sales pitch. Your job is to deal with these issues before you get to the closing stage so they are non-issues at that point.

Prospecting – this is the act of finding potential clients. There are many ways to prospect and a good strategy is to use a combination.

Sales Strategy – this is the process you create to go through the steps necessary to land a sale. From defining the value of your product/service to identifying your target market, to creating your marketing material, to prospecting, actual selling and then closing, your sales strategy is comprised of the 'hows' in each step.

Strategic Alliance – this is a specific relationship with a company in an industry that is complementary to yours. It is a relationship with someone who is marketing directly to your prospect base, hears the problem that your product/service solves, and can refer you in. In addition, you can do the same for him. This is a relationship that is nurtured constantly, and where the referring goes in both directions.

Target Marketing – this is marketing directly to a specific prospect pool. When you know the value of your product/service, the problem that it solves, then you know who has that problem. These are the people you target in your marketing and prospecting.

Value – this is the reason people buy your product/service. It is the elements of your product/service that either solve a problem or prevent a problem. Why do people buy it? And why do they buy it from you? When you know the answers, you'll know the value of your product/service.

About The Author

As a child, I didn't just have a lemonade stand – I had a candy and beverage business. From there I graduated to running a babysitting/summer day camp when I was 14 years old. From setting up the structure to recruiting customers to the daily operations, it was business at its best.

After graduating from Michigan State University with a B.S. in Social Science, I spent the majority of my adult work life in management and sales with small, privately held businesses. From Supervisor to Director of Operations, I have successfully grown teams of people in manufacturing and service companies. I've conducted employee orientations and trainings. Throughout my sales career, I've bested the quotas set by management. More importantly, I've developed invaluable relationships with customers and peers. I excel at networking and believe that relationship building is the key to sales success.

As a certified, professional coach, I work with people in career transition, people wanting to start their own business, salespeople who need and want to improve their skills, and business owners who feel something lacking in their staff's performance. I help businesses and organizations operate more constructively and profitably. As a professional coach, I evaluate, encourage, and guide my clients. Working with as few as one person to as many as 100+, I create an environment that is cooperative and interactive.

My coaching style is centered on learning about you, the client; your strengths, goals, values, and challenges. Together we develop and implement a plan that will help you succeed.

- President of Seize This Day Coaching www.seizethisdaycoaching.com
- Co-Founder of Seize True Success www.seizetruesuccess.com
- Contributing author to Chicken Soup for the Soul: Power MOMS
- Contributing author to www.examiner.com
- Member of Top Sales Experts www.topsalesexperts.com
- Editor for COSE Mindspring – a free online resource for small business owners www.cosemindspring.com
- Cleveland Coach Federation President-Elect
- Lakewood Chamber of Commerce Board Member
- The Business Exchange Chapter Leader

CPSIA information can be obtained
at www.ICGtesting.com
Printed in the USA
FFHW021353300519
52731548-58246FF

9 780981 800462